Raya

Praise for the Book

'An exemplary biography that brings the whole world of Vijayanagara to life as no previous book has ever before succeeded in doing. Minutely researched, full of new material with apparently effortless command over primary sources in multiple languages, this finely written study of the great king Krishnadevaraya is full of good stories, revealing anecdotes and cleverly analysed myths. It makes an excellent introduction to the history of Vijayanagara and should be required reading for all visitors to Hampi.' **William Dalrymple**

'Though reigning for a mere twenty years at the start of the sixteenth century, Krishnadevaraya became synonymous with the aura of the Vijayanagara empire, with Tirupati (the world's richest temple today) and with the Telugu language. But as a man Raya has remained almost completely elusive until this riveting study.' **Rajmohan Gandhi**

'Srinivas Reddy's *Raya* offers a vivid and engaging account of the life and brilliance of the mighty Krishnadevaraya and chronicles with great clarity the charisma, force and vision with which he would establish the powerful Vijayanagara empire – a glorious period of our history whose rich legacy lives on to this day.' **Shashi Tharoor**

'In this unique biography of Krishnadevaraya, Srinivas Reddy captures the interests both of the general reader and of the specialist historian. He uses an impressive array of primary sources, liberally quoting from them to preserve their distinct textures and flavours. Periodically the narrative opens up to discuss broader issues of overarching importance, such as the nature of courtly culture and debates in the historiography of Vijayanagara. His argument that Krishnadevaraya's real nemesis was not any of the Muslim sultans of the northern Deccan, but rather the Hindu Gajapati ruler Prataparudra is compelling and original. That Reddy manages to harmonize all this is a testament to the unifying quality of his engaging narrative. The book is a must-read for anyone interested in Indian history.' **Phillip B. Wagoner**

'Impeccably researched . . . a thoroughly enjoyable, intelligent, altogether edifying biography that combines academic sophistication with good writing.' ***Mint***

'A book that lovers of history could consider pouncing upon.' ***Scroll***

'A compelling, disciplined and compact biography . . . [Reddy's] use of primary sources ... is extremely valuable.' ***Frontline***

'Well-written, absorbing ... It gives us a clear picture of a personality who had a huge impact on the shape of India.' ***Deccan Herald***

Raya

Krishnadevaraya of Vijayanagara

Srinivas Reddy

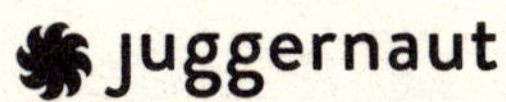

JUGGERNAUT BOOKS
C-I-128, First Floor, Sangam Vihar, Near Holi Chowk,
New Delhi 110080, India

First published in hardback by Juggernaut Books 2020
Published in paperback by Juggernaut Books 2024

10 9 8 7 6 5 4 3 2 1

P-ISBN: 9789353453350
E-ISBN: 9789353450984

Typeset in Adobe Caslon Pro by R. Ajith Kumar, Noida

Printed at Thomson Press India Ltd

for

Professor Padmanabh S. Jaini

quidquid agunt homines, votum, timor, ira, voluptas
gaudia, discursus, nostri farrago libelli est.

Whatever things occupy people – their desires and fears,
their angers and pleasures, their joys and runnings about –
they become the medley of our little book.

Juvenal, *Satires I.I.85–6*

vijayanagara-vṛttāntamu
sujanalache vinnayaṭṭi sūnṛta-vākyul
prajalaku teṭapaḍaṅgā
sṛjiyiñciti kṛṣṇrāya śekharu-carital

So that the people may clearly know
the history of Vijayanagara,
I have put together the deeds of King Krishnaraya,
in true and pleasing words
that one might hear from virtuous men.

Rāyavācakamu I.1

Contents

Prologue xi
Note on Sources xvii
Map xx

Part I

1. Coronation 3
2. The Early Days 18
3. The Medieval Deccan 30
4. The Expanding Empire 40
5 Bijapur and the Sultans 48

Part II

6. The Eastern Mountain 63
7. Tirupati and Temples 74
8. Kondavidu Fort 80
9. Rival Kings 94
10. The Lion Mountain 102

Part III

11. Court of Culture 117
12. Road to Raichur 128
13. Battle on the Krishna 140
14. City and Palace 152
15. The Final Years 163

Bibliography 177
Notes 185
A Note on the Author 233

Prologue

In the winter of 1515, a mighty army pitched camp along the banks of the Krishna river, deep in the heart of Telugu country. Meanwhile, their trusted leader quietly made his way to a nearby temple where locals worshipped a regional form of Lord Vishnu. It was the sacred Vaishnava day of Ekadashi, and King Krishnadevaraya of Vijayanagara fasted with devotion before laying his head to rest in the temple's sacred cloisters. It was the eve of the young Tulu king's greatest battle, and that night he had a dream that would forever change his life, and the fate of his people.

The benevolent god Andhra Mahavishnu appeared before the king – his lustrous black body was cloaked in golden silk, his wide open eyes were bright as lotus flowers, and the Kaustubha gem on his chest was a deeper red than the rising sun. The king was awestruck and humbled as god himself spoke to him in a gentle but serious tone:

'You've already written works in Sanskrit, but now you must compose an epic poem in Telugu, the language of the people! Tell the story of Andal and my wedding in Srirangam, for though I am a Telugu king and you are the king of Kannada, Vishnu is one and the same for everyone. Do this for my glory and your future will grow brighter and brighter with each passing day!' And with these prophetic words, Andhra Mahavishnu disappeared into the darkness.

Early the next morning Krishnadevaraya awoke astonished. He performed all the rituals with deep devotion and offered his salutations to the central temple spire. Next he called together all his priests and soothsayers and related his most wondrous dream. The assembly was amazed to hear of the god's visitation and assured the king that the auspicious vision meant certain victory. Lord Vishnu himself was commanding a king of Karnataka to write about a Tamil saint in classical Telugu! Krishnadevaraya thus felt perfectly capable of uniting the whole of south India under his inclusive banner. And so, with this divine mandate in his heart, the young king rallied his men together and set out to face his most hated enemy.

His arch-rival was not one of the five Bahmani sultans who continued to harass the empire's northern border, but rather the Gajapati king Prataparudradeva of Kalinga.

This proud king now controlled many key strongholds south of the river Krishna, and Krishnadevaraya was determined to reclaim them for Vijayanagara. The deep animosity between the two Hindu kings had been boiling for years – Prataparudradeva was a blue-blooded kshatriya, born into a long line of Solar dynasty kings, and Krishnadevaraya was but a low-caste upstart from humble origins. Prataparudradeva lorded it over Krishnadevaraya; he insulted him whenever he could by calling him a *dasi-putra*, the son of a servant girl, and never once saw him as an equal. The piercing taunts had worked, and Krishnadevaraya now marched with unrelenting resolve to humble his haughty rival. He knew in his heart that he was a great king, Lord Vishnu believed it too, and Krishnadevaraya was determined to prove his mettle to the world.

~

Today, Krishnadevaraya of Vijayanagara is remembered as the iconic king of south India. Most histories portray him as a Hindu warrior who crushed Muslim invaders, some paint him as a peasant who rose to become an emperor, and yet others remember him as a shrewd statesman, a brilliant poet or a benevolent ruler. Each of these identities contributed to the king's remarkable persona, but he was much more than any one of these readings. What makes Krishnadevaraya so exciting is that his life embodies all the vibrant dynamism of his era, a time that witnessed radical transformations in the social, cultural and political life of South Asia, and the world at large. His two-decade reign from 1509 to 1529 falls in what scholars call the early modern period, a precipice of world history when new global networks were being forged – cultures merged and cultures clashed, but the vast lands of the earth were not yet claimed by European colonialism. Krishnadevaraya thus represents a critical transformation from ancient king to modern politician. And in that sense, he was India's first global leader. He had to confront very modern problems such as building international alliances and negotiating overseas trade deals while grappling with the challenges of globalism and multiculturalism. The Deccan of his time was a place where Hindus and Muslims, north Indians and south Indians, Persians and Portuguese, all intermingled as they made their lives and fortunes.

In the eyes of the world, Vijayanagara was the epitome of oriental opulence. It was a cosmopolitan metropolis, the best provided city of the world, more magnificent than Rome, and so exceedingly rich that diamonds were traded in the streets by the basket load! And at the height of the empire's glory there ruled a magnificent monarch, the most feared and perfect king that could ever be! The myths surrounding Krishnadevaraya began in his own lifetime, nurtured by sycophantic court poets, horse-trading Portuguese chroniclers and travelling storytellers. But myths are not antithetical to the discipline of history; indeed, they are critical components of how history is made and why it is propagated. Disentangling fact from fiction is but one part of historical research, contextualizing and interpreting that material is another part, for good history is not the pursuit of an absolute truth, but rather a search for meaning.

The legends of Krishnadevaraya's exploits spread widely after his death, but he consciously set them in motion, particularly through his *Amuktamalyada*, a glorious epic poem that the king did in fact compose in honour of Andhra Mahavishnu. That fateful dream of 1515 was no mere fiction – it was divine inspiration for an unforgettable empire.

This book is just one telling of Krishnadevaraya's life. It is based on the available historical archives, but it listens with sympathy to the legends, songs and memories of people. I was first enchanted by Krishnadevaraya when I read the remarkable poetry of his *Amuktamalyada*. Although literary texts like these are often viewed as works of pure imagination, rarely if ever mined as historical sources, I believe a sensitive reading of such material gives us a unique window into a poet's mind, and in this case, the spirit of a great king. With this array of materials, I have tried, in the most genuine way I can, to present Krishnadevaraya as he might have seen himself, at the very heart of a magnificent world.

Note on Sources

Most histories of the Vijayanagara empire and its famous kings have been told through the eyes of foreigners. The hard facts and figures of much of the Indian past were recorded in the words of hundreds of travellers, explorers and merchants who visited India from all around the world. Many wrote about south India, including Moroccan scholar Ibn Battuta (d.1377), Italian merchant Niccolo de Conti (d.1469), Russian merchant Athanasius Nikitin (d.1472), Persian court chronicler Abdul Razzaq (d.1482), Italian traveller Ludovico di Varthema (d.1517) and Portuguese officer Duarte Barbosa (d.1521). In regard to Vijayanagara's history, our most extensive written sources remain the chronicles of Domingo Paes and Fernão Nunes, two Portuguese horse merchants who both spent time in the Vijayanagara capital during its heyday. Each of these travellers wrote accounts of their wondrous experiences in India, and though they contain much detail, they must be read, like all historical sources, keeping in mind a text's context and pretext.

Although it has been argued that India did not have a tradition of historical writing, for millennia Indians have recorded their past in creative ways, through sculpture, inscription, myth, poetry and song. These sources may be deemed soft in the hard discipline of history, but if read in the right light, they offer fascinating historical insights found nowhere else. In addition to Persian histories like the *Tarikh-i-Ferishta* written by Bijapuri historian Ferishta and the *Burhan-i-Ma'asir* by Sayyid Ali Tabataba, I refer to Telugu literary sources such as the *Rayavacakamu*, a unique seventeenth-century historical text, along with various Telugu court epics like the *Manu Caritramu* of Peddana, the *Parijata Apaharanamu* of Timmana and, most importantly, Krishnadevaraya's own literary masterpiece, *Amuktamalyada*. Sensitively reading each source with respect to its context, its production, its author and its intended audience offers us vivid perspectives into the medieval south Indian past.

We thus have before us a remarkable array of materials: archaeological remains, multilingual inscriptions in stone and copper, European travel literature, Persian *tarikhas*, Portuguese court chronicles, epic poetry, genealogies, local *kaifiyats*, folk songs, oral verses and popular legends. These sources are generally laid out on a linear spectrum with some deemed more scientific, objective and factual while others more artistic, subjective and fanciful. I have tried to avoid this polarization by reading each source in context and putting disparate sources in conversation with each other. This, I believe, gives us a rich and holistic picture of the king and his time.

One demand of stitching together various source materials is the need to reconcile the staggering variety of names, dates and events. Multiple chronologies have been made uniform so the reader can smoothly follow the events of the king's life. In addition, certain quotations have been slightly modified for grammar and flow. In some instances I have left certain terms as they appear in the original text or translation in order to retain some of the historical texture of each given source. For example, Portuguese sources call Muslims Moors, while Hindu sources use Turks or Yavanas. In other sources Hindus are referred to as heathens, infidels and gentiles. The interested reader can refer to the notes for more details.

Lastly, Krishnadevaraya is referred to by many names and epithets throughout these sources. In his own time he was known as Krishnaraya, but today most people simply call him Raya, the king. They do so out of affection and pride as they carry a living memory of the king and his glorious exploits. I grew up listening to those stories, and I draw upon them now as yet another source of history.

SOUTH INDIA AND THE DECCAN
EARLY 16TH CENTURY
Godavari
AHMEDNAGAR
CUTTAK
GAJAPATIS
BAHMANIS
Simhachalam
BIDAR
Warangal
GOLCONDA
Gulbarga
BIJAPUR
Kondapalli
Krishna
Raichur
Kondavidu
Andhra Mahavishnu
GOA
Mudgal
Ahobilam
VIJAYANAGARA
Udayagiri
Tungabhadra
VIJAYANAGARA
Penukonda
Tirupati
Chandragiri
Indian
Ocean
Srirangapatnam
Shivasamudram
Chidambaram
Kaveri
Sri Villiputtur
SRI
LANKA
CAPITAL
Temple
Fort
©Zac Culbreth 2019

Part I

1

Coronation

In the modern-day village of Hampi, across from a pillared assembly hall in an ancient Shiva temple built on the southern bank of the meandering Tungabhadra river, rests a stone tablet inscribed with poetic lines in Sanskrit and medieval Kannada. The slab was installed to commemorate the coronation of a young and hopeful new king. It relates that in the Shalivahana-Shaka year 1430, on the fourteenth day of the bright half of the month of Magha, a festival was held in celebration of Krishnadevaraya's coronation, when he granted the village of Singinayakanahalli to the Shiva temple so that it might provide sweet fruits and cakes to Lord Virupaksha. The new king of kings also donated a golden lotus set with the nine precious gems, a golden vessel, two ceremonial drums and twenty-four silver lamps to be used for the evening arati. And lastly, he had a new mandapa built inside the temple, the very assembly hall that still stands today. The inscription dates to 24 January 1510 and was installed months after the coronation. And although precise dating remains a challenge for Indian history, general chronologies are indeed possible. The evidence makes clear that Krishnadevaraya, a young man in his early twenties, ascended to the Lion Throne of Vijayanagara in late 1509 and celebrated his official coronation in early 1510.

To put things in a global perspective, this was around the time of Henry VIII's enthronement as the king of England, Shah Ismail's conquest of greater Persia, Michelangelo's painting of the Sistine Chapel, Montezuma's dominion over the Aztec empire and Afonso de Albuquerque's capture of Goa. To be sure, it was a dynamic and often turbulent time in human history when unprecedented global connections (and conflicts) heralded the dawn of a new world order. At the same time, remarkable advances in technology, art, science and literature reinvigorated ancient traditions with a modern, cosmopolitan vitality. For example, ancient political wisdom from Kautilya's Sanskrit text *Arthashastra* was reformulated by medieval poets (like the king himself) in vernacular languages to accommodate new and localized political realities. And so, for a young king like Krishnadevaraya, the inescapable past was not to be forgotten, but rather remade as the foundation for a bright and promising future.

The Hampi inscription begins with some thirty Sanskrit verses that describe the mythical genealogy of Krishnadevaraya's legendary predecessors. By claiming descent from the moon, the Vijayanagara kings imagined themselves as part of the fabled Lunar Lineage, putting them in league with celebrated kings like Pururavas, mighty warriors like Arjuna and wise sages like Vishwamitra. This kind of genealogical grafting was a common practice among medieval Indian dynasties, particularly new royal families who sought to legitimize their ancestral right to rule. Krishnadevaraya's poet laureate Allasani Peddana later put it this way: 'In the beginning, rising from the depths of the Milky Ocean, came the Moon, that King of Stars and Light of Heaven. And to the Moon was born a son, versed in the Vedas, whose name was Budha. And to him was born the mythological king Pururavas who had the courage of a lion. And his son was Ayus whose son was Yayati.' And with his first wife Devayani, Yayati had two legendary sons: Yadu and Turvasu. Krishnadevaraya was part of the Tuluva dynasty and claimed descent from Turvasu. Interestingly, the earlier Sangama dynasty kings of Vijayanagara traced their ancestry back to Yadu. Peddana craftily adds that Turvasu was the better of the two brothers, having a wealth of good qualities and much fame. This slight change was a clever strategy that allowed for continuity with the Lunar Lineage while accommodating a distinct dynasty with an alternative pedigree. Indeed, these well-crafted mythical genealogies validated newly minted royals by connecting them to a revered, albeit mythic, historical lineage.

Krishnadevaraya's Tuluva dynasty was the third dynasty to rule over Vijayanagara. Earlier in the mid-fourteenth century, the brothers Harihara and Bukka founded the empire and established the Sangama dynasty that held sway for a solid century and a half. By the late fifteenth century, however, Vijayanagara, which had by that point grown into a powerful empire commanding large swathes of southern India, was in turmoil. Repeated incursions from neighbouring kingdoms, internal rebellions and a string of weak kings had left the empire precariously unstable. The last two decades of the fifteenth century witnessed two usurpations of the throne and multiple short-lived reigns by rulers from three separate dynastic families. During this volatile period in the history of Vijayanagara, the founding Sangama dynasty collapsed, the transitory Saluva dynasty came and went and the powerful new Tuluva dynasty rose to prominence.

Most Tuluva genealogies conveniently skip over this tumultuous chapter of dynastic succession and narrate how Turvasu's descendants established a lineage in which many famous kings were born. One of them was the semi-historical Timma, a powerful king whose strong arms bore the weight of the world and brought stability to it. To him was born Ishvara, a handsome and noble-minded lord who protected the righteous. And to him and his virtuous wife Bukkamamba was born Narasa, the first real-life king of the Tuluva dynasty who ruled the world and made it sinless. And so, in a smooth and seamless manner, the genealogy of Krishnadevaraya's ancestors moved from mythical to historical.

By all accounts, Narasa Nayaka was a fiercely effective general who served during the Saluva interregnum. The Hampi inscription proclaims that he conquered many enemies: the southern empires of the Chola, Chera and Pandya lords, along with many brave Turks and the kings of Kalinga. But Narasa Nayaka was unlike his predecessors from the other two dynasties; he is believed to have hailed from the Tulu country, a coastal region of southern Karnataka with a distinct language, history and culture all its own. It was perhaps the similarity between 'Tuluva' and 'Turvasu' that prompted these kings to attach themselves to this mythic ancestor, but regardless, two things become clear: one, Narasa Nayaka was an upstart from outside the inner circle of ruling Vijayanagara elites, and two, he was not a kshatriya by birth. He was most probably from a shudra background, but his bravery in battle and strong leadership enabled him to seize the Lion Throne and save the empire from collapse.

The inscription continues: 'Just as Rama and Lakshmana were born to King Dasaratha by his queens Kausalya and Sumitra, two brave but modest sons, prince Viranarasimha and Krishnaraya were born to King Narasa by his queens Tippamba and Nagalamba.' By most accounts, Krishnadevaraya's elder brother Viranarasimha ascended the throne after their father for a short but praiseworthy reign. Peddana declares that Viranarasimha killed all his mighty enemies with the worn blade of his terrifying sword, while the Hampi inscription praises his generous ritual donations to all the great shrines and temples of the south. It was after his five-year reign that the young Krishnadevaraya finally became king of Vijayanagara in late 1509.

Royal successions were often fraught with intrigue and complication, and there are many versions of how Krishnadevaraya ascended the throne. While most histories attest to the reign of Viranarasimha, folk legends suggest that Narasa Nayaka passed the mantle of kingship directly to his younger son. One legend claims that Viranarasimha's mother Tippamba hatched an assassination plot against her stepson. Luckily the ever-watchful minister Timmarasu spirited the young Krishnadevaraya away and kept him safe from such court intrigues. Upon Krishnadevaraya's return, when Narasa Nayaka was finally on his deathbed, the ailing king called his two sons to his side and said, 'Whichever one of you can pry this signet ring from my hand shall inherit the throne.' And being the elder of the two, Viranarasimha tried first, but to no avail; no matter how hard he tried, the ring would not slip from the old king's swollen finger. It was then that Krishnadevaraya, seeing that there was no way to pry the ring off, unsheathed his dagger and sliced off his father's finger. The dying king was unfazed; in fact he was pleased, knowing well that his successor would be a man of fearless action.

This somewhat gruesome tale resembles the apocryphal story of Alexander the Great and the Gordian knot. As the legend goes, there was a huge tangled knot, made of hundreds of smaller knots, in the town of Gordium where a prophecy proclaimed that whoever could unravel the great knot would become king of Asia. And so when young Alexander arrived in Gordium en route to India, he didn't try to untangle each knot one by one like all the others; he simply sliced through them all with one swift sword stroke! These tales conjure up images of brash young kings who could achieve what others deemed impossible. Krishnadevaraya and Alexander were men of resolve, and they knew their destinies would have to be forged with bold actions. Another less bloody story is told of Narasa

Nayaka's test for his two sons: in a spacious hall the king had a large carpet laid out, and in the middle of it he placed a dagger. Then he challenged his sons to retrieve the dagger without stepping on the carpet. Viranarasimha tried and failed, but Krishnadevaraya simply fell to his knees, rolled up the carpet, and grasped the dagger. Although we cannot take these tales to be factual, they encode specific qualities of Krishnadevaraya's personality – he was bold, decisive and clever.

Most historical accounts, however, maintain that Krishnadevaraya took the throne after his elder brother's reign. Fernão Nunes, who was in Vijayanagara from 1535 to 1537 collecting stories from locals, relates the following: When Viranarasimha was sick on his deathbed, he called his minister Timmarasu to his side, along with his eight-year-old son, the heir apparent. He then gave two commands to Timmarasu: first, to raise the young boy to the throne upon his death, and second, to put out the eyes of his younger brother Krishnadevaraya and bring them to him as evidence. Timmarasu reluctantly consented and departed. He called for Krishnadevaraya and took him aside to a stable and revealed to him his brother's plan. Krishnadevaraya said, 'I do not wish to be king, nor anything else in the kingdom, even though it should come to me by right. I only desire to pass through this world as a yogi.' Hearing these noble words, and seeing that Krishnadevaraya was an able man of over twenty years and therefore more fit to be king than his boy nephew, Timmarasu commanded a she-goat to be brought before him so that he could have its eyes put out. Then he presented the goat's eyes to Viranarasimha so the king might die thinking his will was done. And as soon as Viranarasimha had passed, Timmarasu raised Krishnadevaraya to the Lion Throne of Vijayanagara.

This dramatic tale might contain a kernel of truth, and like the other stories, it tells us about Krishnadevaraya's spiritual inclinations, as well as Timmarasu's importance throughout his life. A final account of the king's ascension comes from the *Rayavacakamu*, a seventeenth-century semi-historical text that presents us with a detailed, albeit imagined, account of the proceedings of the fateful day when Viranarasimha freely abdicated the Lion Throne of Vijayanagara. While seated in the great hall, Viranarasimha turned to his military commanders and said, 'Indeed, the time has come to pass this diadem on to Krishnaraya. Besides, I am growing old, so it is only fitting that officers be appointed to perform his coronation so that he may begin to rule the kingdom.' And finding an auspicious moment, Viranarasimha named his younger brother Krishnadevaraya successor to the Lion Throne of Vijayanagara and presented him with the signet ring of the kingdom.

The text goes on to describe all the court officials and military commanders who came together for the occasion, notably Timmarasu, the venerable minister who was lovingly addressed as Appaji, along with his son and his grandson. Also present were the official clerk, the state treasurer, several local chiefs and feudatories, scholars, priests, poets, astrologers and many other people both young and old. At the auspicious hour all of them helped give Krishnadevaraya a ritual bath, exactly as prescribed in the sacred texts. Then they seated him in a golden seat on a ceremonial dais, where he performed the sixteen great donations and other meritorious acts. He donated mountains of gold, silver, jewels and pearls, gifted millions of cows and granted support to a thousand families. Water was brought in golden vases from the four oceans and from all the great rivers: the Ganga, Yamuna, Saraswati, Narmada, Sindhu, Kaveri and Tamraparni. Then, at the precisely ordained moment, the air resounding with the sound of horns, tabors, conches, kettledrums and gongs, a group of brahmans anointed the king with those sacred waters as they chanted Vedic mantras. They showered him with gold and heaps of the nine precious gems: rubies, pearls, red corals, emeralds, yellow sapphires, diamonds, blue sapphires, garnets and beryls. Then they dressed him in fresh clothes, perfumed him with the finest sandalwood scents and draped him in a yellow shawl as if he were Lord Vishnu himself! And after that a grand feast was enjoyed by all of Krishnadevaraya's family, closest friends and personal attendants. When the meal was over, Krishnadevaraya washed his hands and rinsed his mouth with scented water.

A folk story is told about the momentous occasion when Timmarasu raised the young Krishnadevaraya to the throne. Right before the ceremony, Timmarasu called Krishnadevaraya aside and instead of imparting some secret advice or personal praise, he slapped the would-be king across the face. Krishnadevaraya was shocked and taken aback, but then he reflected on Appaji's strange behaviour, for he knew there was a lesson to be learned here. Timmarasu explained how important it was going to be for the young king to remember the hardships of life and the pain of being punished. As a final teaching, he advised that punishments ought to be meted out judiciously, for after this day Timmarasu would be unable to discipline his new king, only obey his command, whatever it may be.

When the official ceremonies were finally completed, Krishnadevaraya seated himself on a multicoloured carpet and summoned Appaji and his other ministers and commanders. He explained that since he was a young king, he needed to be instructed in the protocols of court and the proper conduct of a king. To this the ministers replied, 'First of all you should know that the king of the Lion Throne is none other than an emanation of Vishnu.' And then they recited a verse on royal conduct:

> When a man is youthful, and adorned with the nine gems,
> fragrant flowers and perfume, and served by leaders of men,
> he is rightfully called a king, the Lord of the Great Hall.
>
> And for a man loved by the goddess of wealth, a generous hero,
> radiant as a treasury of virtues, look to the Lion Throne
> in the Great Hall, and the victorious king who rises to fill it!'

They continued their advice with a long list of precisely itemized directives: 'The one who sits on the Lion Throne should understand the seven constituents of the state: king, minister, ally, treasury, country, fort and army. He should know the seven gifts of honor: palanquin, fine clothes, ornaments, vehicles, royal favors, camphor and pan. He should know the seven techniques for dealing with an enemy: conciliation, sowing dissension, bribery, attack, deceit, overlooking transgressions, and trickery in war. And the seven royal vices: women, dice, drink, the hunt, arrogance in words, harshness in war and wasteful spending.' And in this way, Krishnadevaraya's learned ministers went on to enumerate an extensive list of political maxims that a wise king ought to know, understand and put into practice. In short, they advised the king to 'punish the wicked and protect the good', for a 'king's success depends entirely on his ability to live according to dharma'. These often dry catalogues of political injunctions were more than mere abstractions to Krishnadevaraya; he listened to them carefully, filling his mind and heart with this traditional wisdom. Indeed, these theories of governance would find practical expression throughout his reign.

Upon receiving these important teachings on governance, the new king inquired about how to acquire wealth for the empire. The assembled advisers explained, 'If the king acts in accordance with dharma, the rains will fall at least three times every month and make the earth most fertile. If the palace then takes taxes that are its due without being unjust, the palace will prosper, and great quantities of money will flow into the treasury.' And then they offered a verse from the famous Telugu political theorist Baddena:

> Justice is the way to make the people prosper
> and the people's prosperity is the way to wealth,
> that's why they say: justice is the true treasury of kings!

Krishnadevaraya listened carefully to all the sage counsel offered by his advisers and said, 'Until now, my brother and father have ruled the kingdom. Now I must go and see all the kingdoms, forts, lands, citadels, temples and sacred places that have been under their power.' Appaji and the others agreed. 'Yes, the king should personally inspect the realms ruled by his predecessors. If you just stay where you are, then you'll never learn anything about the business of the kingdom. You should go and let your subjects behold you. To impress your enemies and feudatories, you should go with your terrifying army to inspect the eight directions and make your fame shine!'

Krishnadevaraya was pleased with these words and resolved to go and see all the lands of his realm. But first he decided to send out spies so he could find out about the different regions of the realm, the strengths and weaknesses of the local lords and chiefs, the various villages and towns and what the people, both learned and simple, were saying about him. The new king was keen to understand the greater world around him, and his returning spies only confirmed what he had already expected: support from his southern base was weak, the Gajapati lord of Orissa was quickly eating up the empire's eastern realms and the prickly sultans to the north, particularly the Adil Shah of Bijapur, was ever hostile. But this situation was also the perfect opportunity for a young new sovereign to exercise his will and establish his might. And so, at the end of the day, the young king Krishnadevaraya took his seat on the Lion Throne of Vijayanagara and looked out to his vast empire with both hope and determination.

2

The Early Days

Krishnadevaraya employed a cadre of spies to gauge the pulse of his people. His agents were fast of foot, strong in mind, fluent in many languages and skilled in the art of disguise. But their reports were not enough for the adventurous young king who often went out on his own intelligence gathering missions. At night, after all his official duties were complete, he would disguise himself and slip out of the palace under the cover of darkness. Interestingly (and unlike most other premodern South Asian monarchs), we have an eyewitness record of Krishnadevaraya's physique. Domingo Paes was granted an audience with the king and observed him at close quarters. Contrary to Krishnadevaraya's popular image today as tall, dark and handsome, and in stark contrast to his likeness in the Tirupati bronze seen on the cover of this book, Paes describes the king as being 'of medium height, and of fair complexion and good figure, rather fat than thin', with signs of smallpox on his face. However he may have looked, popular legends tell us that the king would often dispense with his richly embroidered silks and don the garb of a common man so that he might roam the city streets and observe the people of his capital in secret. Then, right at the break of dawn, he would sneak back to his chambers and rest a while before starting his day at sunrise. The king would brush his teeth and wash his face, and after he had applied his devotional mark and sipped some sacred water, he would enter the great hall. Remembering all the things that he had seen and heard during the night, he would turn to Jangayya, his chief of security, and ask what had transpired at night. The king would listen carefully as Jangayya gave his report, and if all was in accordance with what he had observed himself, he would remain happy and quiet.

In addition to reconnaissance, Krishnadevaraya was probably going out to meet Chinnadevi, a beautiful and talented young dancer he had fallen in love with before becoming king. According to Nunes, when Krishnadevaraya was young and growing up in the city of Vijayanagara, he had a secret liaison with a courtesan for whom he had much affection. And out of his great love for her, he promised her many times over that he would marry her should he become king. Chinnadevi was not from a royal family; she was a low-caste dancing girl, and as king he could not take such a woman as his principal wife. But as the stories go, he loved her dearly and would steal out of the palace at night so they could be together. On the way to one such evening tryst, he was discovered by Timmarasu, who followed him all the way to Chinnadevi's house. The old minister rebuked the young king as he accompanied him back to the palace, but all the while Krishnadevaraya professed his genuine love for her and told him of his promise. Understanding the king's genuine affection for Chinnadevi, Timmarasu gave way to his wish, and promised to marry them in secret. But first Timmarasu oversaw Krishnadevaraya's marriage to Tirumaladevi, a royal princess from the Tamil country who would be the king's principal queen. Only then did Timmarasu arrange for the king's second marriage to Chinnadevi. She would remain the king's true love throughout his life, the queen he adored above all others.

During those early days at court, Krishnadevaraya came to realize something critically important: the Vijayanagara state system of oath-bound lords and vassals had grown precariously weak. His brother Viranarasimha seemed to have let things slip; morale had ebbed, and the new king found an inadequate army in defence of the capital. He needed to rectify this situation at home before dealing with any rebelling feudatories or enemy kings further afield. The nayaka system as it was practised was a type of Indian feudalism: various *nayakas* (lords) pledged fealty, along with monetary and military resources to the king, who in turn guaranteed protection and support to the lords and their people. These arrangements were held together by an abiding loyalty to the king, the heart and soul of the realm. As long as a nayaka paid an annual tribute and maintained a requisite number of soldiers, horses and elephants, he was granted full autonomy over his allotted territory. The nayaka's standing army was always ready for immediate action, for the king could call on them at any time to fight a battle. Any failure on the nayaka's part led to instant ejection, as the king was lord of all. In north India there was the comparable *iqta* system of feudal governance, first implemented during the Delhi Sultanate period, and further refined and expanded under Mughal rule. There are clear overlaps between medieval European feudalism, the north Indian iqta system and the south Indian nayaka system, but comparisons between these fluid forms of governance remain superficial. The common core of these systems was reciprocity: an underlying equation of shared power between state and sovereign on one side and locality and lord on the other.

One revealing incident told in the *Rayavacakamu*

speaks of Krishnadevaraya's clever plan to galvanize his lords, as well as Timmarasu's equally shrewd assistance in effecting it. It began one morning as the king was listening to the recitation of stanzas on royal conduct. He heard a poem by Baddena that struck him deeply:

> Only when a king has an army greater than his lords
> will he grow strong enough to secure the authority
> needed to deploy his forces far and wide.

Krishnadevaraya immediately summoned all the palace accountants and treasurers and asked them, 'How much revenue comes to the Lion Throne of Vijayanagara from the provinces? How many forts and citadels are there in the kingdom? How many cities and villages are there, and how much cultivated land?' And then he commanded, 'I want you all to prepare detailed figures for our holdings in coin, precious ornaments and jewels; for the savings treasury; for the accounts from district temple superintendents; and for the palace's salaried forces, including elephants, horses, and their attendants.' Allalanatha, the keeper of the treasury, replied apologetically, 'All these days, king Viranarasimha never once inquired about the details of the accounts. But, now that my Lord has shown an interest in these matters, I will gladly prepare the figures you have requested.' And after carefully working all day and night, Allalanatha submitted a detailed financial report. He said, 'By my calculations, the *nayaka* estates ought to provide the king a standing army of 24,000 horses, 1,200 elephants, and 200,000 infantrymen. But the *nayakas* have continually failed to provide the correct number of horses, elephants, and infantrymen. This disparity is certainly worthy of your majesty's consideration.'

The young king was stunned by this disturbing report; his lords had larger armies than his own! Krishnadevaraya turned to his ministers for advice, but they all bowed their heads in silence. Finally Timmarasu spoke up, saying, 'Don't worry, we'll run things to your satisfaction, your lordship needn't say another word.' This upset the king even more, for he felt inconsequential and powerless, unable to act independently among his ministers. He mulled this over for a long time, and then one night, as he slipped out to make his rounds, Krishnadevaraya escaped to a temple some leagues north of the city. He was determined not to return to the palace and spent the night there in secret. In the morning, Timmarasu was alarmed not to find the king in his chambers. He quickly sent spies off in every direction with instructions to find the king and report back to him. And soon enough, one spy returned and informed the minister of the king's whereabouts. When he heard this, Timmarasu sent written messages to all the lords, nobles and chief nayakas, telling them that the king had decided to go hunting, and that they should all come quickly with their full forces. And so they hurried about and made ready their men, and as soon as everyone had gathered – all the horsemen, elephant riders, infantrymen, retainers, nobles and lords present in the city – they sallied forth with Timmarasu at the head. Once they crossed the city walls, Timmarasu ordered the men to fall in rank, get into formation and stay at the ready. Then he dismounted and made his way to the temple where Krishnadevaraya was waiting.

A cordial exchange of grievances sprinkled with pleasantries passed between king and minister, until Krishnadevaraya finally expressed his pressing desire for a strong standing army, along with the funds required to pay them all a proper salary. Timmarasu replied that he would ensure this happened right away and quickly summoned the troops gathered nearby. Right then and there, with the palace accountants by his side, Timmarasu made public all the discrepancies in both the military and monetary tribute due to the state by the lords present. Shamed and remorseful, the lords immediately offered to their king 500 elephants, 12,000 horses and 1,00,000 infantrymen from their own ranks. And so, just like that, the wise old Timmarasu turned the king's wish into reality. Krishnadevaraya was amazed! He exclaimed, 'Who else but you has the power to make the impossible

possible?' He ordered Timmarasu to be presented with the seven worthy gifts: a cap, an ornamental shirt, a necklace, a pair of pearl earrings, a yellow shawl, fragrant musk and paan. 'Indeed,' rejoiced the king, 'today at last my kingship has been set on firm ground!' The king mounted his elephant named Masti Madahasti and climbed into the golden howdah. He called upon Timmarasu to take the seat behind him, and king and minister triumphantly marched back to the capital with a mighty new army following close behind.

This unique story reveals several important themes related to a stable government: the critical importance of a salaried army stationed in the capital, the loyalty and goodwill of lords, a strong-willed king and a clever minister. The *Rayavacakamu* adds that when Krishnadevaraya returned to the palace, he boasted to his retainers, 'Is there any other minister in this world who is like my Appaji Saluva Timmarasu? Just look at what can be done when you have a minister like Appaji!' And indeed they would accomplish much together, for the man who was like a father to the young king would prove to be Krishnadevaraya's fiercest ally and most trusted adviser.

One verse written by the king himself echoes what he believed were the qualifications of an effective minister. It is more than evident that Appaji was the inspiration for it, and perhaps the poem even lends credence to the eventful day described above.

A learned brahman, versed in statecraft
    and horrified by injustice,
older than fifty but younger than seventy,
    devoid of ego and from a healthy family,
who only takes up the office of minister
    at the behest of the king, will discharge
his duties successfully, and in just one day,
    strengthen every branch of the government.

The enumerated attributes fit Timmarasu perfectly. By most accounts he hailed from a Telugu-speaking Niyogi family of brahmans who took up secular vocations rather than priestly ones. And by the time of Krishnadevaraya's ascension, Timmarasu was probably in his early fifties, having dutifully served in ministerial posts under both Krishnadevaraya's older brother and father. An inscription from the Tirupati temple complex highlights his generosity, erudition and brahmanic pedigree. It ends with a praise poem: 'May the glorious minister Timmana, whose mind is like a bee forever worshipping the lotus feet of Srinivasa, be victorious as long as the moon and stars shall shine!' An oral verse attributed to the late Vijayanagara poet Ramarajabhushana describes Timmarasu as a self-made man from humble origins. In his youth he earned a living stitching leaf plates, then he travelled from place to place, surviving on alms and living in boarding houses. Finally he secured the post of betel-bag bearer to the commanders of various forts, and ultimately he rose to become prime minister of the whole kingdom. Though apocryphal, the verse speaks to Timmarasu's unswerving grit and ingenuity.

Timmarasu's importance and influence at court was further strengthened by the loyal support of several family members: his son, grandson and two nephews were all trusted advisers close to Krishnadevaraya. The king's inner circle was thus packed with the old minister's faithfuls. In fact one of Timmarasu's nephews was also his son-in-law, for the common practice of first-cousin marriage served only to strengthen and consolidate the powerful blood ties of this influential family. And so the man Krishnadevaraya always lovingly addressed as Appaji, respected father, would remain the most powerful and influential man at court. As Paes put it, Krishnadevaraya's 'greatest favorite is an old man called Timmarasu; he commands the whole household, and to him all the great lords act as to the king'.

The fact that many brahmans of the period were taking up employment outside of their traditional role as teachers and ritual specialists was a reflection of the increasing social mobility and diversification of occupations in medieval South Asia, and particularly in the Deccan. Traditionally exclusive kshatriya positions such as lord, vassal and officer were quickly being taken up by local shudras like the king himself, while enterprising brahmans increasingly became ministers, strategists and fort commanders. It was a dynamic time when individuals from various backgrounds increasingly found new opportunities and employment in the expanding Vijayanagara state system. As Cynthia Talbot's study of medieval Telugu inscriptions reveals, the medieval Deccan exhibited 'a level of physical and social mobility not found in older localities as well as a large degree of fluidity in the configuration of political power'. In that sense the volatility of the Deccan's political climate created new spaces for social mobility in regard to place, occupation and status.

In reference to his brahman officers, Krishnadevaraya advised: 'Entrust your forts to loyal brahmans alone. Give them the bolt to the gate, and grant them unrestricted local authority so that fear arises in the enemy. There is no limit to implementing this policy.' And indeed he promoted this practice throughout the kingdom, praising brahman fort commanders as 'loyal, well educated, righteous and brave', adding that 'with a brahman at the head of a fort, a king can sleep peacefully with his hand resting gently on his heart'. Even Paes noted the variety in brahman occupations when he wrote, 'These brahmans are like friars with us, and they count them as holy men –

I speak of the brahman priests and the lettered men – because the king has other brahmans, many are officers of towns and cities and belong to the government.' The diversity of Krishnadevaraya's administration mirrored the social vibrancy of the premodern Deccan. The social and political landscape was changing all around him and Krishnadevaraya embraced this new potential for the vast empire he now commanded.

3

The Medieval Deccan

Before moving to the events of the king's early reign, we must acquaint ourselves with the history of Vijayanagara, and its place in the dynamic socio-political milieu of the medieval Deccan. Krishnadevaraya inherited an expansive kingdom, soon to be the largest and most powerful political entity to ever command the southern subcontinent, but its roots were much humbler.

Until the early fourteenth century, four major empires ruled the lands south of the Vindhyas: the Yadavas at Devagiri (Maharashtra), the Kakatiyas at Warangal (Telangana), the Hoysalas at Dvarasamudra (Karnataka) and the Pandyas at Madurai (Tamil Nadu). Infighting within each empire made for a precarious political landscape. Adding to the instability was the mounting threat posed by the great sultan of Delhi, Alauddin

Khilji, who charged his fearless general Malik Kafur to attack, pillage and subjugate the south. Indeed, it was the first time in history that the rulers of Delhi were able to penetrate into the south. All four of the great southern empires suffered the brutal northern onslaught. From 1308 to 1311, Malik Kafur and his men battered the south: they ploughed through the Yadavas and Kakatiyas in the Deccan, marched right over the Hoysalas in Karnataka and sacked the Pandya city of Rameshwaram at the very southern tip of India. Alauddin Khilji's bid to control the south turned the region into a battlefield; the Deccan became the heart of the bitter power struggle between north and south India.

Vijayanagara was born out of these volatile circumstances, and the kingdom's fabled origin story contains within itself both the promise of greatness and the omen of ruin. It is a tale of two brothers, a sacred geography and one legendary sage. With the ultimate disintegration of the Kakatiya empire in 1323, local chieftains and community groups, like the Reddys of Kondavidu and the Velamas of eastern Telangana, rose in power. From one of these local warrior groups came two brothers, Harihara and Bukka, whose adventures would lead to the founding of the city of Vijayanagara. The brothers began their careers in the service of the Kakatiya king Prataparudra. But when his capital of

Warangal fell, Harihara and Bukka fled to the abandoned Hoysala stronghold of Kampili on the Tungabhadra river, some twenty kilometres downstream from the future site of Vijayanagara. When Kampili also fell to the Delhi Sultanate just four years later, the brothers were taken as prisoners to Delhi, where, according to some accounts, they converted to Islam and ingratiated themselves with the sultan. As reward, they were dispatched back to the Deccan to quell a local uprising and rule over the newly incorporated territories on behalf of the sultan. The story goes that once back in the south, the brothers quickly rejected Islam, proclaimed their independence and went on to establish the new Hindu kingdom of Vijayanagara.

This is but one version of the Vijayanagara origin story, but as historian Phillip Wagoner states, 'everything about the story, from its language to its narrative structure, suggests that it must not be read as a record of religious conversion' but as a key component in the political legitimization of Vijayanagara's founding. The point of the story is to illustrate that Harihara and Bukka were no upstarts, they had an official mandate from the great sultan in Delhi. As historian M.R. Rao adds, the brothers Harihara and Bukka 'embraced Islam as a measure of expediency', perhaps to save their lives but more as a means of furthering their careers. Thus, the tale tells us more about political authority than religious conviction, and affirms that Vijayanagara was influenced by Islamic political culture from its very origin.

The realm that the upstart brothers had claimed for themselves was the mythical land of Kishkindha: ancient home of legendary monkey warriors of the *Ramayana* like Vali, Sugriva and Hanuman. There, across the arid plains flows the river Pampa or Tungabhadra, gently coursing its way through barren expanses and breathtaking clusters of gargantuan boulders that appear to float in the sky. As historian Anila Verghese explains, 'The Tungabhadra river afforded natural protection on the north and the west, while the dramatic landscape of hillocks and rocky outcrops created a vast natural fortress.' Harihara and Bukka's vision for their new dominion wasn't something preconceived, it arose from the rugged terrain before them, just as the city they would go on to build would seem to magically emerge from the rocky landscape.

Generations of myths and legends about Kishkindha had imbued the land with sacred power. In particular, many holy places from the *Ramayana* dot the rugged landscape: Sita's bathing lake, Anjanadri hill where Hanuman was born, Shabari's ashram and Mount Rishyamuka where Sugriva once lived with Rama. But well before this epic/Puranic layer of myth, locals venerated the land, particularly the river goddess Pampa who was worshipped in the area for centuries. As was common throughout the subcontinent, local village deities were often absorbed and incorporated into the Puranic pantheon. One way this was done was by celebrating the marriage of a local goddess with one of the two main gods, Vishnu or Shiva. In this case, Pampa became the consort of Shiva in his form as the three-eyed Virupaksha. According to Pampa's new cosmic origins, she was the daughter of Brahma who performed severe penance and won over Lord Shiva the ascetic. Even today the most important festivals at the Pampa/Virupaksha temple in Hampi are the *phalapuja* (betrothal) and the *kalyanotsava* (marriage festival).

It was in this sacred land that Harihara and Bukka set out to establish their new capital. As the story goes, one day the brothers set out on a hunt and witnessed a most unusual sight: a hare chasing after a hound. According to Nunes, they were astonished to see such a feeble creature biting a dog, and they were convinced that it was some kind of omen. In fact this trope, which conveys an inversion of the natural order, figures in the origin myths of many medieval Indian cities, like the Bahmani sultan Ahmad Shah's founding of Bidar, Ahmad Shah of Gujarat's establishment of Ahmedabad, and Sala's rescue of his Jain guru at the Hoysala capital of Shashakapura, 'City of the Hare'. The brothers needed guidance to decipher the true meaning of the omen so they ventured closer to where the chase took place, at the base of the sacred Mount Matanga. And as they approached they saw a holy man, radiant and glowing with the light of knowledge. The man was the scholar-sage Vidyaranya, meaning Forest of Learning, and he explained, 'According to the sacred traditions of this place, it's impossible for anyone – no matter how strong he might be – to harm the weak here. It's because of the curse of the great sage Matanga. A long time ago, the mighty monkey king Vali lived in Kishkindha with his younger brother Sugriva. Once they had a fight and Sugriva ran away to this hill. The invincible king Vali came chasing right behind him, but the great sage Matanga cursed Vali so he couldn't climb up the hill. And ever since that time, no strong fellow – whether animal or man – has been able to do his strong man's business up there! So you see, no matter how strong someone is, when he comes to this place, he ends up powerless.'

Harihara and Bukka were amazed and inspired by the sage's story; they were convinced that this was the perfect spot for their new capital. According to legend, Vidyaranya's mentor had urged him to circumambulate the earth and visit the holy city of Kashi. Vidyaranya made his way to Kashi where he met the legendary Vedavyasa who told him, 'You will establish a city in Karnataka. The auspicious glances of Lakshmi, goddess of fortune, will continue to fall on that city for three hundred and sixty years. And there will flourish a line of thirty kings, occupants of the Lion Throne, who will be renowned for their fame, and you must be their preceptor for as long as the city exists.' And with these words the venerable Vedavyasa disappeared.

Vedavyasa's prediction excited the young Vidyaranya, but he also knew the prophecy contained a time limit – the new city would flourish, but only for 360 years under thirty kings; Vijayanagara's glory was thus forever tied to its downfall. Regardless, Vidyaranya proceeded back to the banks of the Pampa from Kashi where he waited for the fated arrival of Harihara and Bukka. The day finally came when two brothers in search of a new city met a wise sage destined to build one. Vidyaranya thus became the royal purohit and spiritual guide to Harihara and Bukka, and advised them on the proper construction of the new city. In honour of the sage, the capital was originally called Vidyanagara, the City of Wisdom, but soon it would be known to the world as Vijayanagara, the City of Victory. Indeed, this transition from wisdom to victory speaks to the rapid expansion of the future empire.

Later chronicles like the *Rayavacakamu* insist that the empire's power ultimately derived from Vijayanagara's specific location. The sacred power of the spot was enough to protect the capital, and the great empire to be. And so in 1336, Harihara was enthroned by Vidyaranya in the new capital and became the founding ruler of the Sangama lineage, and the first king of Vijayanagara. Like many polities of this time, Vijayanagara was a regional empire with transregional aspirations. It was founded and ruled not by elite kshatriya nobles, but by enterprising local leaders with strong regional ties. The next century and a half witnessed many kings, some noble and heroic, others ineffective and unsung. Regardless, by the time of Krishnadevaraya's ascension in 1509, the empire had expanded greatly and held sway over the southern subcontinent, from the Krishna river down to Rameshwaram. The geopolitical landscape had also shifted, and new powers to the east and north challenged the expansive but tenuously held realm.

Along the eastern seaboard, the Gajapati kingdom was quickly amassing new land and gaining more power. King Kapilendradeva, founder of the Suryvamsi kings of Orissa, established the empire in 1434 and expanded it over the next thirty years to encompass all of Orissa, parts of Bengal and much of the Andhra country. His successor Purushottamadeva strengthened the empire's holdings, which kept him in constant conflict with the kings of Vijayanagara who claimed ancestral sovereignty over much of the conquered territory south of the river Krishna. This mounting antagonism would reach a climax during the reign of Krishnadevaraya who would take it upon himself to reclaim the contested lands. He would fight the longest campaign of his life against King Prataparudradeva, the last of the great Gajapati sovereigns.

Along its northern border, Vijayanagara had to contend with the Bahmanis, a conglomeration of Deccan sultans founded in the wake of the disintegrating Delhi Sultanate. Muhammad Tughlaq, who ruled over Delhi in the early fourteenth century, had ambitions to conquer the south and in 1327 decreed that the imperial capital would be shifted to the erstwhile Yadava capital of Devagiri in the Deccan. The city was renamed Daulatabad and the entire Delhi court was begrudgingly compelled to make the long trek of over a thousand kilometres. The move proved challenging to say the least and the new capital was fraught with various difficulties from water scarcity to regional rebellions. In 1347, while Harihara was already ruling as king of Vijayanagara, Muhammad Tughlaq was forced to move his capital back to Delhi. A revolt in Daulatabad led by a regional general named Alauddin Bahman Shah from Afghanistan led to the formation of the Bahmani sultanate, the first independent Muslim sovereignty in the Deccan. But even this configuration would prove tenuous, and by the late fifteenth century when Vijayanagara was experiencing its own dynastic shifts, the Bahmani sultanate had all but splintered into five distinct kingdoms: the Nizam Shahis of Ahmadnagar, the Qutb Shahis of

Golconda, the Barid Shahis of Bidar, the Imad Shahis of Berar and the Adil Shahis of Bijapur, collectively known as the Deccan sultanates. They continued to pledge an empty fealty to Mahmud Shah, the token Bahmani sultan, but by the time of Krishnadevaraya's ascension, each sultan was fiercely exerting his autonomy. And so, as Bahmani power was dispersing, Vijayanagara power was being consolidated.

Of the five independent Deccan sultanates, it was Bijapur, whose realm bordered Vijayanagara's northern front, that Krishnadevaraya would engage with most directly. The fact that Bijapur (from the Sanskrit Vijayapura) also means City of Victory underscores the notion that these rivals shared more in common than is generally accepted. In fact, they were cognates in more than name alone. Vijayanagara and Bijapur, like most polities that thrived in that era, were upstart kingdoms; they were born from the volatile geopolitical milieu of the medieval Deccan where empires rose and fell, and loyalties swayed with the wind. Just a century before Krishnadevaraya's rule, the Bahmani sultan Feroze Shah married a princess of Vijayanagara as a pledge of allegiance. It was an exciting, albeit turbulent time to say the least, and the feeling that one could chart their own destiny created the perfect environment for the enterprising young Krishnadevaraya. He had rightfully claimed the Lion Throne of Vijayanagara, and now he was determined to lead it to glory.

4

The Expanding Empire

Around this time, one other critical player entered Deccani politics: the Portuguese. Since Vasco da Gama's arrival in Kerala in 1498, the Portuguese steadily solidified their control over Indian Ocean merchant networks by capturing critical trade centres like Hormuz in the Middle East and Malacca near modern-day Singapore. In 1509, under the relentless command of Admiral Afonso de Albuquerque, Portuguese forces stormed the city of Calicut while its king, the Samorin, was engaged in internal disputes further inland with the raja of Cochin. The city was in ruins and eighty Portuguese lives were lost, for which Albuquerque was 'determined to exact vengeance'. He wrote to the king of Vijayanagara who he believed was hostile to the Samorin, and promised that if Krishnadevaraya would 'come with his army by land, he Afonso, would come by sea, and together they would destroy the Samorin'. With this end in view, Albuquerque dispatched to Vijayanagara one Friar Luis of the order of St Francis with a letter of instruction that read as follows: 'Tell the king Krishnadevaraya of the glory and power of my lord, the king of Portugal, and of the great fleets which he sends every year to India, and how the Indian seas are only sailable and safe because of him. And likewise, tell him how the king of Portugal commands me to render honour and willing service to all the gentile kings of his land. They are to be treated well; we shall take neither their ships nor their merchandise. But I am to destroy the Moors, with whom I wage incessant war. I am prepared and ready to help Krishnadevaraya with the fleets and armies of Portugal, but he must help us with his army, towns, harbours, and munitions, and whatever else I may require from his kingdom.' And so Albuquerque's stratagem of conquest was simple: pit local polities against each other and exploit native hostilities to further Portugal's imperialist agenda. It was a technique he used often, and to good effect, but it wouldn't prove effective on Krishnadevaraya, at least not yet. And so, in late 1509, around the time of Krishnadevaraya's ascension to the throne, Friar Luis set out north along the coast from Cochin to Bhatkal, and from there proceeded by well-trodden hill paths to Vijayanagara to give the king this message.

Friar Luis's reception at the Vijayanagara court was hardly cordial. He was made to wait for weeks before being granted an audience. It was around this time, in early 1510, some sixty leagues (around 300 kilometres) due west of Vijayanagara on the Indian Ocean, that Albuquerque took the port city of Goa from Bijapur. Earlier the port of Goa was under Vijayanagara control, and so it was always a territory of some dispute between the two kingdoms. Now a third party had entered the fray and Krishnadevaraya was cautious not to jump into a hasty alliance. This is how Albuquerque described Goa: 'This harbour was always the principal passage to the kingdom of Vijayanagara and the Deccan; and for this reason it contains much merchandise, and large caravans from the interior of the country that transport and sell commodities. From this commerce the inhabitants of Goa have grown prosperous.' Albuquerque clearly saw the economic and political value of Goa and he was quick to capitalize on the sentiments and ambitions of native rulers.

At this historical moment, warhorses imported by sea from West Asia were the most sought-after imperial commodity. And since indigenous horse breeds were not hardy enough for warfare, sturdier foreign horses were constantly being imported into the subcontinent. Albuquerque and the Portuguese had seized control of Middle East ports like Hormuz and Aden, and so they could channel all foreign horse imports to Goa and monopolize the South Asian overseas horse trade. The overland horse trade into the Deccan 'had virtually ceased ever since the Bahmanis revolted against their former Tughluq overlords a century earlier. As a result, horses could no longer be brought to the Deccan overland from Central Asia and north India, but had to be shipped across the Arabian Sea.' It was this lucrative trade network that the Portuguese sought to control exclusively.

In a letter to his sovereign, King Dom Manuel, Albuquerque wrote, 'Because the king of Vijayanagara wants to secure a steady supply of horses to his land, he will do whatever you request. With Goa in your power, the kings of Vijayanagara and the Deccan will both pay tribute.' And in another letter to his king, Albuquerque boasted: 'I have determined that all the horses from Arabia and Persia should be in your hand. First in order to receive the high duties paid on horses, and second because the kings of Vijayanagara and the Deccan will strive for peace with you. They see that you have the power to give them victory over each other, because without doubt, whoever has the horses from Arabia and Persia will win.' Thus the ascendancy of the Portuguese in India was tightly linked to war and horses; it was nothing short of a medieval arms race.

Krishnadevaraya grasped this new reality but it was still

too early for him to fall in league with the Portuguese. Friar Luis sought an alliance with him against the Samorin of Calicut, but this was a king with whom Vijayanagara had no quarrel. Only later would Krishnadevaraya favour the Portuguese and try to seek exclusive access to the all-important warhorses they traded in. In a verse he would write years later, he advises that foreign merchants ought to be housed in mansions and treated lavishly. For the moment, however, Friar Luis does not seem to have been provided such luxurious accommodations, nor were his overtures met with an enthusiastic reception. In fact most sources record that Friar Luis was murdered under mysterious circumstances before being able to return to Albuquerque. Other sources add that Krishnadevaraya listened carefully to the friar's message and dispatched a diplomatic party to Albuquerque, along with explicit instructions to the envoys not to commit themselves too far. As one writer put it, 'He adopted a policy of diplomatic prolongation of negotiations,' or in a word, he stalled. Krishnadevaraya had other plans in mind, and this was not the time to commit to an unknown new ally. For now he had more pressing matters to attend to closer to home. And though the first encounter between Vijayanagara and the Portuguese started off a bit cold, it would later flower into a more cordial and mutually beneficial relationship.

Around the time Friar Luis was at court, there erupted

a revolt in the southern principality of Ummattur, near modern-day Mysore. This was one of many minor rebellions brewing in the southern reaches of the empire, an area that had perpetually maintained a tenuous allegiance to Vijayanagara. Whenever the centre seemed weak, or in transition, like now when a new king had just been installed, polities in the south would exercise their claims of independence. One such rebel was the Gangaraja of Ummattur whose father Tyaparaja had unsuccessfully battled against Krishnadevaraya's brother Viranarasimha. Their claim to sovereignty was made as follows: 'We have been ruling this country from time immemorial. Our ancestors, have ruled this country for a long time, we never paid tribute to any other king. Your father Narasa Nayaka conquered us by force of arms and exacted tribute from us. We are under no obligation to pay you tribute, and we will send you nothing.' With a young new king on the throne of Vijayanagara, the Gangaraja seized the opportunity to capture the fort of Penukonda, a long-time Vijayanagara stronghold.

This brazen attack on a key Vijayanagara position was too much for Krishnadevaraya to let stand. For the first time since his enthronement, he was ready and willing to dispatch forces. With a small but sizeable force of 5,000 infantrymen and 2,000 cavalry, Krishnadevaraya marched south towards Penukonda. Upon reaching the stronghold, the king's forces 'surrounded and suffocated it, capturing the place in just one day'. The fortress was seized and its walls razed to the ground. Krishnadevaraya left some loyal officers in charge and headed on to the famed island fortress of Sivasamudram. Also under the control of the Gangaraja, it was positioned in the middle of the Kaveri river and flanked by the twin hills of Pretaparvata and Gevuruyana. It was a formidable target, and Krishnadevaraya knew he had to dig in for a long siege. According to local sources, the king's army encamped all around the fortress and 'blockaded all passage to the fort by way of the Kaveri for over a year'. Finally, as the court poet Timmana records, the fort walls came toppling down into the blood-red waters of the Kaveri. In desperation, the Gangaraja drowned himself in the waters of the river that had until then protected him.

From Sivasamudram Krishnadevaraya 'marched on to the fort at Srirangapatnam, where he inspected the ramparts and bastions, and worshipped the Lord Adi Ranganayaka'. This famous island fortress, which was in rebel alliance with the Gangaraja, readily capitulated to Vijayanagara sovereignty as well. The command of these retaken southern forts was granted to known and trusted Telugu lords, rather than local Kannada or Tamil lords, because Krishnadevaraya was confident these men would remain loyal to him. Indeed, it was their proven loyalty, not their Teluguness, that the king sought. The idea was that their presence would bring a degree of peace and security to the southern empire. Krishnadevaraya stabilized the south by filling top administrative positions with Telugu loyalists from his inner circle. And to further secure the young king's dominion over the deep south, Timmarasu arranged for Krishnadevaraya's marriage to Tirumaladevi, the daughter of Kumara Vijaya, the defeated lord of Srirangapatnam. The new alliance would prove essential for Krishnadevaraya, both personally and politically. Although we have little historical information about the queen, tradition maintains that she was a strong-willed royal woman, jealous of the king's love for Chinnadevi, but confident in her public position as queen of the empire. Her central position at court cemented relations between the new king of Vijayanagara and his powerful southern allies. Tirumaladevi would remain Krishnadevaraya's devoted chief queen throughout his reign, and never again would his southern base rise up in rebellion. The 'whole of the south' had submitted to Krishnadevaraya and he returned to his capital to celebrate his first victory, and his royal wedding.

5

Bijapur and the Sultans

After the king's return to Vijayanagara, the historical record becomes somewhat muddled. Nonetheless, we can be certain that sometime in 1511, somewhere between Raichur and Gulbarga, Vijayanagara and its historical rival, the Adil Shahis of Bijapur, met in battle. The circumstances of the confrontation remain unclear but a cobbling together of various sources gives us a sense of the context and tone of the bitter engagement.

According to historian R. Subrahmanyam, the spies that Krishnadevaraya had deployed to all corners of his realm were coming back with new intel. Those returning from Bijapur informed him that 'some insolent words' were uttered by the sultan of Bijapur. This greatly irritated Krishnadevaraya and he immediately ordered his troops to assemble. And with clear intent to chastise the Adil

Shah, he set out at the head of his forces towards Bijapur. This may seem hasty, but Krishnadevaraya was known for his temper; he could easily flare up, especially if he felt insulted in some way. Even at this young age his impulsive nature was evident, but it would only be later in life that this rage would prove tragic. At this point, Krishnadevaraya's reaction was surely due to the historical animosity that had been building for decades between the two cities of victory.

According to the Persian court chronicler Ferishta, during the reign of Krishnadevaraya's father Narasa Nayaka, the sultan of Bijapur sent a message to Vijayanagara entreating peace, 'upon which Narasa Nayaka came, attended by three or four hundred nobles, to a conference in the field, where Yusuf Adil Shah of Bijapur fell upon them by surprise with his whole army and killed seventy persons of rank. Alarmed at the death of their chiefs, the troops fled, and were left to be plundered by the victors.' The memory of this betrayal, unrecorded in Hindu sources, likely spurred the king's call to arms.

And so in 1511, Krishnadevaraya set out to face the man who had nearly killed his own father. According to the *Rayavacakamu*, the king approached the Krishna river, which was Vijayanagara's traditional northern boundary, but he was shocked to find that the forces of Bijapur (aided by the forces of Ahmadnagar and Golconda) had already forded the river and ensconced themselves in Vijayanagara territory. The sultans had 'already sallied forth and crossed the river. They began digging trenches and setting up' the symbolic Battle Tent that was a signal of attack. According to Islamic sources, the sultans marched to the Vijayanagara border 'in accordance with the policy of annual jihad against the Hindu infidels inaugurated by the Bahmani ruler Mahmud Shah'. Tensions were high and Krishnadevaraya was 'furious', but he was unsure of his next move.

It was then that an influential Telugu lord named Pemmasani Ramalingama Nayadu suggested a plan. He explained that the Battle Tent set up by the sultans signalled an offensive – the enemy was dug in with an intent 'to fight to the finish'. Ramalingama then rallied 'nobles of his own Kamma caste' to lead a daring, dangerous mission to attack the enemy front with the express mission of cutting the ropes of the Battle Tent, a symbolic gesture that would strike a devastating blow to the enemy's morale. Ramalingama 'jumped and danced about excitedly to urge the men on. Leaving their hopes and worries behind eighty thousand soldiers came forward like anxious bridegrooms. Each of them felt like they were marching off to a waiting bride!' Spotting Ramalingama's strike, the sultans mobilized their troops, cavalry and elephants to guard the Battle Tent. As Ramalingama and his men approached the camp they 'dismounted and jumped with their swords and shields onto the backs of the sultans' elephants. They sported around on top of the elephants like lion cubs frolicking on the slopes of a mountain. They cut the maddened elephants' trunks to pieces, and they pierced the elephant drivers with their spears and made the elephants trample them to death. They lifted the mail off the horses' back and stabbed them with short spears, hafted spears, and pig prods. They sliced them up just like cucumbers, six slices to the blow!'

As the men engaged in a bloody and confused battle, Ramalingama 'cut the tent ropes as he had promised', and at that very moment Krishnadevaraya, who was watching all along, sounded the battle drum and mounted his elephant. On the other side, sultanate forces panicked and began to retreat. Unfortunately, this was the same moment that 'both banks of the Krishna began to swell up in flood. The elephants of the sultans were exhausted from the battle, the heat had built up a tremendous thirst, and as soon as they felt the cool breeze from the rising water, they ran for the river.' Realizing they would be cut off from their reinforcements on the other side of the river, the sultan's forces hastened their retreat to the Krishna's north bank. But just as they were preparing to cross, the river filled with a rushing torrent and the men panicked and tried to flee. Some jumped headlong into the river, but half of them drowned in the swirling waters. The sultans of Bijapur, Ahmadnagar and Golconda quickly dismounted their elephants, got into boats and made their way back across the river. And all the while the elephants calmly quenched their thirst in the middle of the river, and not a soul could make them budge.

But Krishnadevaraya was not satisfied with this victory; he called all his men together and said, 'I want you to ride ahead into the territory of the sultans. Fan out quickly and raid every town within three leagues of the border. I want you to pillage those lands until there is not a single man, cow, sheep, goat or horse remaining. Beat the drums! Strike the tabors! Let the four quarters resound with the sounds of our victory!' And so Vijayanagara troops pillaged every village in the vicinity. They cleaned out grain stores, burned fields and entered every house to pilfer the people's hard-earned savings. It was 'an impressive job of devastating that territory'. War was as it remains today: cruel, indiscriminate and unrelenting.

One significant outcome of this early battle with the Deccan sultans was the death of Bijapur's ageing leader Yusuf Adil Shah. The Persian chronicles are silent about the sultan's demise, recording only that Bijapur 'increased daily in power' as the sultan aged. According to some sources, Krishnadevaraya slew the Adil Shah in the heat of battle and garnered himself the title *paribhuta-suratrana*,

Vanquisher of Sultans. Krishnadevaraya himself penned a vivid praise poem that offers us more explicit detail:

> The fine horses of your cavalry
>   plowed the fields with their hooves,
> and the rushing elephants watered the earth
>   with their downpour of juice.
> Hail Krishna Raya! With a fierce and unified attack,
>   you turned those wild forests into fields of green,
>   spreading your fame like the abundant crops of Kubera!
> You crushed the skulls of Khurasani warriors like melons
>   and built a gruesome effigy
>   with the Adil Khan's decapitated head!

In addition to the graphic image of the beheaded sultan, Krishnadevaraya mentions warriors from Khurasan, or north-eastern Iran. This observation is important because it reveals that the king was keenly aware of the social dynamics in Bijapur. The Deccan sultanates were a unique blend of native, often Sunni Muslims, known as Deccanis, and well-off foreigners from Central Asia and Iran known as Westerners who were 'imported' to court. This Deccani–Westerner split largely paralleled the Sunni–Shia divide at court, and it caused serious political dissension among the Bijapuri elite. Deccanis often felt disenfranchised and passed over for foreign Westerners.

Ferishta records that 'the Deccanis, like wounded vipers, writhing in the torment of jealousy, unitedly resolved on Yusuf Adil Shah's destruction'.

This depiction of a divided Bijapuri court is important to keep in mind when understanding both the religious and political realities of the medieval Deccan. Muslims were never a single, unified group, nor were Hindus. And so any simple polarization of historical events along a Hindu–Muslim divide begs for deeper analysis. Yusuf Adil Shah, for example, was known for his tolerance and inclusive state policies. Ferishta eulogizes him as a 'wise prince, intimately acquainted with human nature; handsome in person, eloquent in speech, and eminent in liberality. He warned his ministers to act with justice and integrity, and always led by example.' One thing that set him apart from the other Deccan sultans was his strong endorsement of Shia Islam. It is recorded that 'shortly after assuming the title of Shah, Yusuf Adil Shah caused the *khutba* to be read in Bijapur in accordance with the tenets of Shia Islam. This was never done before in any part of Hindustan, and the minds of all the Deccanis revolted against him.' But Yusuf was a liberal man and allowed for the free exercise of all religions. His policy was 'my faith for myself, and your faith for yourself'. Ferishta records that people 'lived together in friendship; and in mosques of different sects, each worshipped the true God according to his own belief, without interfering in the ceremonies of the other.' There is no reason to believe this rosy picture to be an exaggeration, for in medieval India religious tolerance far outweighed religious persecution.

In this regard, a story told of one of Krishnadevaraya's predecessors paints a telling picture. King Devaraya of Vijayanagara asked his council why the Muslims were so successful against the Hindus. Some said the Almighty had simply decreed them superior to the Hindus; while others said Muslim superiority was a result of two factors: stronger horses and finer archers. In order to remedy the disparity, Devaraya 'gave orders to enlist Muslims in his service, allotting to them estates, and erecting a mosque for their use in Vijayanagara. He also commanded that no one should molest them in the exercise of their religion, and moreover, he ordered a Koran to be placed before his throne on a rich desk, so that the faithful might perform the ceremony of obeisance in his presence without sinning against their laws.' The anecdote reveals two things: one, that Vijayanagara courtiers were divided in their opinions about religion's role in politics, and two, that premodern leaders had effective strategies to accommodate people of various faiths in their administrations. In the early fifteenth century this same king of Vijayanagara would celebrate his daughter's marriage to the Bahmani sultan Feroze Shah 'amid great rejoicings and princely magnificence'.

A century later, in 1511, Vijayanagara–Bijapur relations were not nearly as cordial. Whatever bonds were forged in the past were now frayed thin and feelings of bigotry were creeping into political life. The *Rayavacakamu*, written a century after Krishnadevaraya's time, reflects a further polarization of these identities. The text records that Krishnadevaraya's ministers spoke of the Bijapuris as 'drunkards with no faith in gods and brahmans. They are barbarians, cow killers.' His most trusted advisers, Ayyamarasu and Kondamarasu, said, 'What are the Turks but drunkards and opium eaters! If someone happens to come in their way, they simply chop him to pieces, they act like demons of the Kali Age!' And to counter the stereotyped characterization, Ferishta writes of Vijayanagara as filled with 'wretches, whose black complexions were but an index of their hearts, giving way to their naturally treacherous dispositions'. But again, such strong comments should not be taken out of context, nor can they be read as indicative of general opinion. The enmity between Vijayanagara and Bijapur was indeed deep, but religion was just one of many factors that shaped the relationship's evolving dynamics.

Much of our current perception about the Deccan and its place in Indian history is rooted in our reliance on colonial-era historical writings that perpetuate certain key formulations. To put it simply, Vijayanagara was cast as the last Hindu empire, bravely protecting India's ancient traditions in the face of imminent Muslim domination. The British civil servant Robert Sewell, in his landmark 1900 publication *A Forgotten Empire* (often considered the first major academic study of Vijayanagara), described the empire's raison d'être this way: 'It was the natural result of the persistent efforts made by the Muhammadans to conquer all of India. When these dreaded invaders reached the Krishna River the Hindus to their south, stricken with terror, combined, and gathered in haste to the new standard which alone seemed to offer some hope of protection. The decayed old states crumbled away into nothingness, and the fighting kings of Vijayanagar became the saviours of the south for two and a half centuries.' This simplified narrative was further echoed and amplified over several decades by both Western and Indian historians. Medieval Indian history was thus repeatedly presented through the lens of a starkly polarizing religious polemic.

Fortunately, more recent histories of Vijayanagara, from scholars such as Richard Eaton, Phillip Wagoner, Manu S. Pillai and others, have endeavoured to highlight the rich complexities that defined Vijayanagara and its multicultural milieu. Wagoner, for example, in his brilliant study of Vijayanagara court attire and royal epithets, argues that 'Hindu culture at Vijayanagara was in fact deeply transformed by its interaction with Islamic culture . . . one begins to recognize the extent to which Islamic-inspired forms and practices altered Indic courtly life in the Vijayanagara period.' His work looks specifically at how Vijayanagara elites took up wearing Islamic courtly attire like the *kullayi* (headdress) and *kabayi* (robes). Wagoner's analysis is based on distinguishing between 'Islamic', which refers to the religion of Islam, and 'Islamicate', which encompasses the social and cultural practices associated with Muslims and Islam. In other words, this formulation conveniently segregates religion from culture and politics, something that is nearly impossible to do, especially in a culture like India's. And although this analytical model is helpful in reformulating and enriching our understanding of Vijayanagara, perhaps the corrective has swung the pendulum too far. One is sometimes left with a feeling that religion had no role to play in the political life of premodern India.

Although we may be tempted to read either communalism or non-communalism into the past, the historical record reveals a much more complicated story. In this regard, Wagoner and others have argued for the need to conceptualize the premodern history of Hindu–Muslim interaction in more than simply religious terms, and to see it as part of a more robust process of cultural interaction. Then as now, however, religion was politicized. Ferishta recounts the story of one Vijayanagara general whose polarizing statements smack of some contemporary political agendas. Bhoj-Mul, a 'maternal relative of the raja, commanded the brahmans to deliver daily discourses on the merits of slaughtering Muslims, in order to excite the zeal of the soldiers. He encouraged the brahmans to arouse their indignation, and confirm their hatred of the enemy, by representing them as temple destroyers, idol smashers, and cow slaughterers.' Divisive statements like these serve political ends; they exploit differences and shift our perspective away from the countless daily acts of tolerance, accommodation and even celebration that diverse communities throughout the subcontinent continue to experience even today.

Chatu poems, or oral verses passed down over the years, tend to memorialize these religious tensions with a lighter tone. One goes like this: 'O Krishnaraya, foremost of heroes! Some of the proud and strong Muslim kings killed by you in battle arrive in heaven and make the gods laugh when they salaam and address the guru Brihaspati as pir, Indra as sultan and Saci as bibi!' Surveying all these sources reveals that one's faith was indeed an important aspect of medieval Indian political life. They also illustrate how religion fanned rather than ignited the burning enmity between rivals like Vijayanagara and Bijapur. And so, when we put all this history into perspective, one axiom becomes abundantly clear: Hindus and Muslims fought among themselves just as much as against each other, and however the battle lines were drawn, they often fought side by side, for each other and against each other. Religion was not *the* dividing line, simply one of the many markers of identity and belongingness that fuelled loyalties, animosities, allegiances and betrayals.

Part II

6

The Eastern Mountain

Now that most rebel uprisings in the south had been quashed, and Yusuf Adil Shah had been silenced in the north, the Vijayanagara capital was more or less stable. Still early in his reign, Krishnadevaraya now turned to the imperial diaries left by his illustrious predecessors. He wanted to familiarize himself with various state policies of past kings as he modelled his own unique vision for the empire. In the course of his study, he came across the words of the heroic Saluva Narasimha, founder of the short-lived Saluva dynasty that preceded Krishnadevaraya's Tuluva dynasty. On his deathbed in 1491 Saluva Narasimha lamented, 'Time has failed me. I desire that my sons, or whoever should inherit this kingdom which I gained by force of arms, should capture the three fortresses that remain in revolt against me still.' One of these was called

Raichur, another Mudgal, and the third was Udayagiri. And since his predecessors had made no progress in retaking these fortresses, Krishnadevaraya 'determined at once to prepare his armies and move against these places'.

Raichur and Mudgal, in the Krishna–Tungabhadra doab, were closer to home and the king would deal with them later, but for now, the most pressing task was to take back Udayagiri and counter the mounting incursions of the powerful Gajapati lord Prataparudradeva. Of all Krishnadevaraya's enemies, this Hindu king, not the Muslim sultans of the Deccan, would pose the longest and most inimical threat to his imperial expansionism. In many ways Prataparudradeva was Krishnadevaraya's arch-nemesis, his doppelgänger, for their similarities far exceeded their differences. Krishnadevaraya's eastern campaign to reclaim lands lost to the Gajapati lasted for six hard-fought years. It was the longest and most sustained military campaign of his life, and it began with the siege of an impregnable fort, perched on the cliff of a rocky peak called Udayagiri, the Eastern Mountain.

From the rocky plains of south-eastern India, a hundred kilometres northwest of modern-day Nellore, rises a high, sheer-faced outcropping, known as the Eastern Mountain, from behind which the sun and moon rise. Covered in thick vegetation and tiny waterfalls, the mountain is topped by a fortified citadel at a height of some 3,000 feet.

Perhaps built in the thirteenth century, the hilltop fort of Udayagiri could only be reached by a single jungle path, at times so steep and narrow that soldiers were forced to ascend its heights in single file. For Krishnadevaraya, taking back this famed stronghold would be strategic as well as symbolic – geographically it marked the southernmost reach of Gajapati power, and historically it was a long-standing bone of contention between the two empires, one that even the mighty warlord Saluva Narasimha failed to reclaim for Vijayanagara.

In the winter of 1512, with a force of 34,000 infantrymen and 800 elephants, Krishnadevaraya set out from Vijayanagara. The king's actual numbers as he departed the capital were surely less than Nunes's estimate, but Krishnadevaraya had a plan. He rallied support along the way, particularly among loyal families at key strongholds, like the fort of Gutti, a medieval structure of Chalukyan times that now housed minor lords of Vijayanagara, or the breathtaking fort atop the gorge at Gandikota, built beside a tight bend in the river Pennar, where wild forests cascade into red granite cliffs. Krishnadevaraya often used marching as a method of bolstering his numbers, as well as his men's morale. He garnered the support of various feudatory families with strategic local ties, like the Aravitis, Toragantis, Gobburis, Nandyalas and Arakus. He believed that when advancing towards enemy territory, a wise king takes his time, starting with a few days of light marching, then slowly adding more and more troops along the way, like a trickle of water growing into an overflowing river.

In late January of 1513, as Krishnadevaraya's united forces came spilling into the rugged Pennar river basin, he quickly dispatched his armies further east towards Udayagiri where they were joined by a local force of another 10,000 foot soldiers and 400 cavalrymen. Krishnadevaraya himself and his personal guard took a detour south in order to seek the blessings of Lord Venkateshwara in the verdant Venkata hills. And so the pious king embarked on the first of his seven pilgrimages to the sacred hill shrine of Tirupati. Along with him were his two wives and a large retinue of retainers. They all travelled south like a moving city on wheels, for every imaginable tradesman, worker, artisan and attendant needed for the king's daily routine was included in the party. And by early February, Krishnadevaraya and his impressive retinue had slowly made their way to the holy Vaishnava temple.

Here the king offered many gifts and paid his respects to Lord Venkateshwara, his *ishta devata* or chosen god, whom he held as the ultimate source and object of his devotion. Krishnadevaraya had come to seek god's blessings on the eve of his greatest military campaign. For him, this simple gesture of devotion sealed his imminent victory. During this same visit, his junior wife Chinnadevi presented a gold cup for offering milk, and his chief queen Tirumaladevi, who hailed from this region and maintained close family ties with the temple, donated another gold cup along with a gold plate used to keep perfumes. Devotion was a family affair, and Krishnadevaraya's initial pilgrimage to Tirupati conjures up one of the first images of the king as a devout and generous man of the people. This image would later be solidified in three magnificent bronze statues of the king flanked by his two wives, and installed in the sacred shrine some four years later near the end of the long Gajapati campaign.

Charged and invigorated by his visit, Krishnadevaraya quickly headed back north to join his main forces already in position around the fort of Udayagiri. Any prospect of storming the citadel by force was all but thwarted by the stronghold's imposing terrain. Even a small force of covert soldiers would have a difficult time scaling the narrow and treacherous path of ascent. A long-drawn-out siege was the only way forward, so the king's only recourse was to wait. Siege warfare involved little to no combat; it was more a battle of wills. Though it would prove long and tiresome, the siege of Udayagiri had a certain end – Krishnadevaraya and his troops were well provisioned, having won the support of local rulers and merchants, while the Gajapati lords, locked away in their mountain citadel, would eventually run out of food and water. Medieval Indian siege warfare was cruel and exhausting. In the end it was sheer starvation that would force a besieged enemy to surrender.

With no real progress in sight, in May of 1513, with the summer heat beating down, Krishnadevaraya escaped to Tirupati, this time without his wives. On this occasion, just a few months after his first visit, he presented gifts to Lord Venkateshwara directly – various jewelled ornaments, ritual swords, tassels, sheaths, armlets and necklaces, along with three *kiritams* (golden crowns) for the processional idols of Venkateshwara and his two consorts Sridevi and Bhudevi. A temple inscription from this time records a benediction in favour of the king's welfare in mythic tones: 'Just as Hari became a Boar to save the Earth, topped by golden Mount Meru like a shining umbrella, may Vishnu's great tusks protect you now!'

Krishnadevaraya stayed for some time and continued his generous gift giving. A month later, as the monsoon rains of 1513 arrived, the king gifted several villages to the temple authorities for the upkeep of the main deity. One day, he departed from Tirupati in the morning, crossed a barren tract around the foot of the Venkata range and offered his evening worship in the hallowed halls at Kalahasti. This temple town is a peaceful pilgrimage site on the banks of the meandering Suvarnamukhari river, receiving far fewer visitors than nearby Tirupati. With a thousand-year-old history layered with Pallava and Chola era structures, this important Shaiva centre was praised in song by generations of Tamil poet-saints. The environs were so conducive to spiritual practice that the celebrated Telugu poet Dhurjati, who was once employed in Vijayanagara as one of Krishnadevaraya's court poets, retired here to lament the depravities of king and court. In one verse he says, 'I've had my fill of sex and pleasure at the palace gates of countless kings, but now I want some peace of mind. O God of Kalahasti, show me a doorway to the highest truth!'

The local form of Shiva here is Srikalahastishvara, whose power brought together the devotion of a spider, a snake and an elephant – *sri-kala-hasti*. On this visit the king gifted many jewels, gold plates and villages to the temple authorities, and likely established the fund that would one day finance an expansion of the central *gopuram*. Here it is important to note that although the king had a fondness for Vishnu, he could easily channel his devotion towards any deity of the Hindu pantheon. Krishnadevaraya's faith, like that of many of his people, was open and non-denominational. Inclusion was at the heart of his Hindu devotion. He believed that all gods were one, that all faiths were equally valid and that every individual was free to choose how and whom to worship. As the Portuguese officer Duarte Barbosa wrote of Vijayanagara in 1518: 'The King allows such freedom that every man may come and go and live according to his own creed, without suffering any annoyance and without enquiry whether he is a Christian, Jew, Muslim or Heathen.' Krishnadevaraya's non-sectarian Hindu faith at a personal level naturally manifested itself as an overarching state policy of tolerance towards all creeds, sects and religions of the realm.

After the monsoon, Krishnadevaraya returned to Udayagiri to oversee the siege that had begun almost six months earlier. Not much had changed. His initial hope was to starve the holdouts into a quick surrender, but Tirumala Rautaraya, a paternal uncle of the Gajapati, and the present fort commander, was well provisioned. He would prove as hard to break as the massive stones that protected him. Under Timmarasu's watchful eye, the men got to splitting huge boulders in the hope of carving out a better way up the rocky crags, but their courageous attempts were met with failure. The fortress was impenetrable, and time was their only ally.

In a phrase, they were stuck between a rock and a hard place: on the one hand was the back-breaking work of penetrating the hard stone walls, and on the other was the mind-numbing waiting for the enemy to surrender. At the foot of Mount Udayagiri was now a small city, stocked with every imaginable provision. 'The camp was very busy with elephants, horses and soldiers in their glittering armour and weapons just milling around. Merchants with bullock carts set up stalls to sell everything: vegetables, grains, clothing, ornaments, fragrances, mattresses and pillows. Barbers, washermen, cobblers, tailors and other tradesmen set up their shops. Delicious dishes of meat and fowl mixed together with tasty spices were served throughout the camp. There was even sweet palm liquor!' But after almost eighteen months of siege life, waiting had grown to frustration, and Krishnadevaraya made a solemn vow to neither eat nor bathe until the fort was taken and the head of his enemy lay at his feet! The Gajapati's uncle and his starving people were already tired and weak. Now fearful of a full-scale attack, Tirumala Rautaraya quickly sent out his turban as a token of submission. The king surely had this moment in mind when he composed this bold verse: 'I, Krishna Raya, supreme lord of the Earth, easily took Udayagiri and seized the Karnata land in my firm arms. The jeweled crown that the Gajapati's uncle offered as a precious gift now lies sparkling at my feet!' The vow itself seems to have been an extreme measure. As the king himself would later advise in another poem: 'A king should be clever, not impulsive. Never make a vow regarding the enemy, for an invasion can drag on and on.' This ability of the king to self-reflect and incorporate the lived experience of his reign into his political theories makes his poems on governance both unique and deeply insightful.

And so, some two years since the plan was first conceived, Krishnadevaraya duly reclaimed Udayagiri for Vijayanagara on 9 June 1514. With Tirumala Rautaraya's surrender also came the seizure of an aunt of the Gajapati, 'who was taken captive but allowed her freedom. She was carried away with all the courtesy that Krishnadevaraya could show her.' She was treated with all the honours due to any senior noblewoman of the king's harem. This policy of respect for royal prisoners, particularly women of nobility, was a crucial component of the king's political strategy, and he would tactfully implement it throughout the Gajapati campaign. After the fort and its environs were secured, the surrounding lands were entrusted to loyal lords under the leadership of a respected local hero known as Kampanna, while command of the fort was given to Udayagiri's new regent, Timmarasu's son Kondamarasu.

As a grand public gesture that resonated both spiritually as well as politically, Krishnadevaraya removed the local Balakrishna idol from the Udayagiri temple of Venugopala with a plan to carry it back to Vijayanagara as a trophy of war. Acts like these were not uncommon nor were they considered irreligious. Some say the removal of the idol was at the insistence of Vyasatirtha, the venerable *raja-guru* of the king, who would soon officiate at the consecration of the idol in a new jewelled mandapam in Vijayanagara. Others saw the act as revenge for an earlier attack on Vijayanagara by the Gajapati's father Purushottama who supposedly carried away a Sakshigopala idol from Vijayanagara. Whatever the case, Krishnadevaraya probably believed this to be an act of retribution; this was a war of vengeance, and the fall of Udayagiri was the first in a string of victories to come.

'When all this was done, Krishnadevaraya called upon Appaji and bade him see, "Look how well I have achieved what Saluva Narasimha had enjoined in his testament! But I'm not content with such a small victory, I want you to march forward a hundred leagues, deep into the kingdom of the Gajapati!"' The king then ordered Appaji to distribute fresh provisions and a bit of gold to all the soldiers. With brimming pockets, the troops under Timmarasu's command now marched northward to the fort at Kondavidu, inside the Gajapati's territory. Krishnadevaraya and his entourage, however, headed home to the capital. All along the way they visited sacred pilgrimage centres, starting of course with his beloved Tirupati. And so just twenty-six days after the fall of Udayagiri, the king was before Lord Venkateshwara to offer his heartfelt gratitude.

7

Tirupati and Temples

The medieval south Indian temple was much more than a house of devotion, it was an institution – a sacred structure at the very centre of public life. Throughout the land, temples both grand and small served as community gathering spaces where cultural programmes were staged, food was distributed and ritual worship was offered from dawn till night. For a large complex like Tirupati, this demanded the employment of thousands of people, from priests, administrators and labourers to dancers, artisans and cooks. Due to the generous land grants of past kings, temple authorities held jurisdiction over large tracts of farmland surrounding the main shrine. The bountiful yield from the rich soil was put to direct use, not only to support the entire temple staff but also to prepare the vast amounts of free *prasadam* to be distributed each day.

The temple was the nexus of south Indian society – it brought the religious, social, cultural and economic life of the community together under one roof of god. There was thus never a division made in premodern India between state and religion, secular and sacred, for such distinctions never existed in daily life. Indeed, the temple was a powerful unifying place, but like all institutions, there were natural hierarchies, and like in all things Indian, caste played its part. As it persists to this day, the inclusion of many perpetuated the exclusion of others. Untouchable devotees, for example, were barred from even approaching some temples. And although Krishnadevaraya was a king now, he remained keenly aware of the social stratification inherent in both the society he governed, and the temple he now honoured.

The origin of the great temple complex at Tirupati–Tirumala is shrouded in myths of aeons past. History tells us that it was lavishly supported by a continuous succession of south Indian dynasties including the Pallavas (ninth century), the Cholas (tenth century) and finally the kings of Vijayanagara. With the advent of the brilliant twelfth-century theologian Ramanuja, Tirupati became a primary centre for the Visishta Advaita philosophy of Sri Vaishnavism, an influential new branch of Vishnu devotion. And by the sixteenth century, the holy shrine was well on its way to securing its current designation as the wealthiest and busiest temple in the world. Today some twenty-five million pilgrims make their way to the hilltop sanctum every year just to glimpse the hallowed black idol of Lord Venkateshwara. After having their *darshanam*, most pilgrims offer, according to their means, some money to the huge *hundi* or donation bag. These daily acts of donation add up to make Tirupati the richest temple complex in the world.

The key to the functioning of the temple was the practice of *dana* or gift giving. Kings donated money, land and gifts to temples, and in turn, the temple's priests conferred divine authority upon the king. It was the same symbiotic brahmana–kshatriya relationship from court being played out in the arena of public devotion. And so, whether it was in the palace or in the temple, the mutual exchange of gifts between kings and priests cemented the reciprocal relationship between state and religion. All along Tirupati's massive stone walls are carved hundreds of inscriptions that bear witness to these acts of charity. These testaments describe (with remarkable precision) the details of each gift, its donor, the intended recipient and the terms of the donation. An inscription that memorialized Krishnadevaraya's first visit to Tirupati reads: 'Hail! On the fifth day of the bright fortnight of the Phalguna month in the year 1434 of the Salivahana Saka era [10 February 1513], Sriman Maharajadhiraja

Rajaparameshwara Sri Krishnaraya Maharaya presented to Lord Venkateshwara a crown set with nine kinds of precious stones, 1,076 units of solid gold for various decorations, 2,822 rubies, 160 emeralds, 423 diamonds, 10 sapphires, one topaz gemstone and 1,339 pearls; along with a three-stringed necklace of blue pearls, two armlets and one broach. All these the donor Krishnaraya Maharaya presented for your decoration.'

Like many of the inscriptions at Tirupati, this one was recorded trilingually, in Telugu, Tamil and Kannada, so that pilgrims from all over the south 'might read them with great zeal since they were written in their mother tongue'. And although most pilgrims in those days were illiterate, they would be sure to at least recognize the distinctive script of their native land. The recording of the inscription in three different languages reminds us that Lord Venkateshwara had followers from across south India. No other southern temple complex garnered such widespread devotion. And so when Krishnadevaraya had his name inscribed on the sacred walls of Tirupati, he was speaking to the whole Dravida country as fellow devotee and king. Inscriptions from the king's extensive pilgrimages and his generous donations to several temples throughout the south mapped a divine empire into the people's memory.

But kings were not alone in their donations. The visit of a monarch was surely cause for pomp and celebration, but dana was practised at the temple all year round, with continuous gifts from local nobles, generals, ministers, guilds, merchants and even some wealthy women. The practice of temple dana was a complex and highly organized system that combined religious piety and charity with land grants and public works projects. Luckily, the trustees of the temple were scrupulous in documenting these major donations, particularly in regard to the exact ingredients needed for the proper preparation of temple food. One of hundreds of inscriptions reads: 'This donation will be used to supply the Sri Bhandaram [temple store] with the following articles: 17 marakkal of rice, 27 nali of ghee, 1,300 palam of jaggery, 1 alakku of pepper, 1 palam of sandalwood, 650 areca nuts and 1,300 betel leaves; in addition to 1 marakkal of green gram, 50 palam of sugar, 20 nalis of curds, cardamom, dried ginger, assorted vegetables and various sauces.' The list is marvellous! It points to an elaborate temple system with precise measurements, strict protocols and an astonishing amount of prasadam!

Whenever Krishnadevaraya visited Tirupati, he brought with him a sizeable entourage of family members, personal guards, attendants and retainers. Almost all of the king's generous gifts came with supplementary donations offered in his name by members of his elite retinue. Both of the king's wives were generous patrons, as was his most trusted minister Timmarasu. In addition, the Tirupati temple inscriptions record fascinating details about the king's inner circle, the people closest to him day and night, who we rarely, if ever, find mention of elsewhere. Individuals like Narasayya, a doorkeeper who offered devotion in the name of his brother and mother. Or Bhaiyappa Nayakar, the king's official betel-nut bearer who 'had to be in attendance upon the royal person at all times'. Or others like Yajna Narayana Bhattar, the king's official ritual priest, Sripati who was the state engraver and personal secretary to the king, and even one Baguri Mallarasa, the king's personal bodyguard. Furthermore, the inscriptions make note of several important women donors, like Lakshmi Ammangar (Timmarasu's wife), Vengalamman and Ekkadi Timmamman, all who gave 'for the merit of Sri Vira Krishnaraya Maharaya'. And when the king gave, so did everyone else around him.

Now, just a month after the surrender of Udayagiri, Krishnadevaraya and his entourage visited Tirupati for the fourth time; they donated lavishly to the temple and offered their heartfelt gratitude to Lord Venkateshwara for his favour and grace. And so, with the pride of victory in his mind and the lord's blessings in his heart, Krishnadevaraya and his party returned home in July of 1514. The city streets exploded with joy as the people of Vijayanagara welcomed their victorious king back to the palace.

8

Kondavidu Fort

While Krishnadevaraya was at home in the capital, his men marched north under the watchful eye of Timmarasu and his able son, Kondamarasu, the newly appointed governor of Udayagiri. After the fall of the supposedly impregnable fort which marked the southern boundary of the Gajapati empire, Krishnadevaraya ordered his men to push north into Andhra country, that fertile delta where the Krishna and Godavari rivers meet the sea. This was the Telugu heartland. Successive generations of local, Telugu-speaking rulers controlled the area and pledged fealty to whichever empire happened to be dominant at the time: Kakatiya, Gajapati or Vijayanagara. Many of them were descendants of local Reddy kings whose sponsorship of Telugu literature, particularly the itinerant poet Srinatha, infused the land with a distinctive cultural identity rooted in the Telugu language. Narayana Rao and David Shulman relate that the poet moved through the delta from patron to patron, kingdom to kingdom, defining the land as a Telugu literary empire. It is thus reasonable to believe that in late 1514, when Vijayanagara forces swept into Andhra with predominantly Telugu-speaking lords and soldiers, they would have been seen by local Telugu residents more as liberators than plunderers.

The primary target of this push was the hilltop fortress of Kondavidu – the Gajapati's southern headquarters and the key stronghold from where several surrounding fortresses were centrally administered. In the words of Srinatha, Kondavidu was 'a temptation and a snare for three kings'. For centuries the fort and its overlords would pass between three great empires of the medieval Deccan: the Bahmani, the Gajapati and Vijayanagara. Kondavidu was the central citadel of coastal Andhra, and whosoever possessed it could claim sovereignty over the land's fertile deltas. Krishnadevaraya was well aware of Kondavidu's fortifications and he knew that a long-drawn-out siege like the one at Udayagiri would grow tiresome. The king's plan was to harass neighbouring forts into capitulation before besieging Kondavidu outright. One of his political maxims even makes reference to such a strategy:

> Just as a farmer occupies new land, by fencing it in,
> digging up rocks and roots, and making it ready for planting,
> a king should occupy a country by attacking an enemy,
> or by taking over forts with bribes. Then he should seek
> and uproot the enemies inside, one by one.

Krishnadevaraya was literally staking out his domain, not so much by ravishing the land, but by reclaiming it as his Telugu base. Timmarasu and Kondamarasu duly put the plan into action and most of the forts around Kondavidu fell with little or no resistance. Although some claim that Vijayanagara forces 'devastated and subjugated the territory', it is more probable that Timmarasu and his family members forged alliances and strengthened their historical ties with the Telugu-speaking Andhra country. At one of the forts, Vinukonda, they wooed the local Sagi chiefs – shudra rulers who rose to power as Gajapati vassals. And at two others, Bellamkonda and Nagarjunakonda, two local Telugu chiefs were made Vijayanagara's local agents. And so through both diplomacy and strength of arms, Timmarasu and his men were able to reclaim the Andhra heartland. With the surrounding hill fortresses under their control, they marched forward with confidence to lay siege to Kondavidu.

It was around this time that Krishnadevaraya and a

new supply of men from Vijayanagara made their way to the eastern battlefront. En route they camped at the sacred temple of Andhra Mahavishnu, a regional form of Vishnu worshipped by local Telugus in the tiny town of Srikakulam on the east bank of the Krishna river. That night, Krishnadevaraya had a dream that would change his life – a visitation from Lord Venkateshwara himself. As he narrates in his *Amuktamalyada*: 'Some time ago I set out on a campaign to expand my empire and conquer the Kalinga country. I marched to Vijayawada with my army and camped in Srikakulam for a few days. There at the temple of Andhra Mahavishnu I worshipped the Lord on his special day of fasting, and then, during the fourth watch of the night, Andhra Mahavishnu appeared to me in a dream – his lustrous black body made the rain clouds look pale, and his bright wide eyes put the lovely lotus to shame; his golden silk clothes outshined Garuḍa's wings, and his Kaustubha gem eclipsed the red rising sun. Lakshmi appeared there too, carrying a lotus in one hand and holding his hand with the other. Her kind face removed all my desires and her gentle smile emanated true compassion.' Andhra Mahavishnu speaks to the king directly, praising him for his mastery of Sanskrit while compelling him to 'create a great poem in Telugu for my pleasure'! He suggests that the king take up the south Indian story of the Tamil poet-saint Andal, because, as he boldly declares, 'I am a Telugu king and you are the king of Karnataka!' And then, as a preemptive measure, he says: 'If you ask, "Why Telugu?" it is because this is Telugu country and I am a Telugu king. Telugu is one of a kind.' And finally, in one of the most oft-quoted lines of regional linguistic identity, the god Andhra Mahavishnu declares: 'After speaking with all the kings that serve you, didn't you realize that among all the regional languages, Telugu is the best!'

These remarkable lines speak to the heart of Krishnadevaraya's inclusive vision for his vast empire, for he was king of Karnataka writing about a Tamil saint in classical Telugu. In fact Andhra Mahavishnu's statements about Telugu are not really linguistic, or even cultural – they are pointedly political in nature. Krishnadevaraya's most trusted lords and generals were Telugu speaking, and the region for which he now fought was home to tens of thousands of Telugu speakers. And although the empire embraced many regional languages, particularly Tamil and Kannada, at this particular moment in south Indian history Telugu was politically dominant, and it was strategically important to align with it. Now the god Andhra Mahavishnu himself was commanding Krishnadevaraya to speak to his base in the language of the land and its people.

After the dream, the king awoke astonished to the

faint light of dawn. He performed all the proper rituals, and with utmost devotion offered his salutations to the central temple spire. 'Early that morning,' the king recalls, 'I summoned wise men and scholars, honored them and related my most wondrous dream. They were amazed and overjoyed. They said, "O Lord! The fact that the God of Gods came to you in a dream foretells a series of auspicious events! Listen! Your devotion will grow stronger, your knowledge of literature will deepen, your treasury will grow even more abundant, and you will become a mighty emperor! You will have many more wives, and many more children, who will live long and uphold the greatness of your glorious Turvasu lineage. These auspicious omens are truly wonderful!"' Inspired by his vivid dream, and filled with energy to reclaim a land that he believed was rightfully his, Krishnadevaraya marched to Kondavidu to join his main forces.

The siege was already in progress, and under Timmarasu's careful command, the fort was completely blockaded. With the newly gained support of local Telugu elites, the Vijayanagara forces were able to ensure that absolutely no supplies entered the besieged citadel. Prince Virabhadra, the Gajapati king Prataparudradeva's son, was the governor. He and several Gajapati loyalists were holed up in the hilltop enclosure. Krishnadevaraya's strategy to attack several forts around Kondavidu had proved effective. The multi-pronged advance had forced Prataparudradeva to disperse his forces, making it ultimately impossible for him to muster a strong enough defence to protect his territories. Nonetheless, when he heard the news that Krishnadevaraya himself had joined the siege at Kondavidu, he made haste to meet his enemy.

According to Nunes, Prataparudradeva sent a massive force to break up the siege: 5,00,000 infantrymen, with 20,000 horses and 1,300 elephants! The numbers are surely exaggerated, and the Gajapati must have engaged Krishnadevaraya with a much smaller force. Prataparudradeva wasn't out for a full-scale battle just yet, but he wanted to show Krishnadevaraya that he wasn't scared of a fight. When the king learned of the Gajapati's approach, he marched out four leagues from the fort and arrived on the south bank of an unidentified coastal river. Halting his army on one side of the river, with Prataparudradeva on the other side, Krishnadevaraya sent a message to the Gajapati: 'If you desire to fight me, then I shall gladly retire two leagues from the river, so that you might cross it unmolested. Once safely across, we may join in battle.' Though the Gajapati gave no reply, he bolstered his position and made ready for battle. Seeing his enemy's determination, Krishnadevaraya charged the river with all his men and elephants. And in the crossing, there were serious injuries to both sides, many were slain.

But Krishnadevaraya managed to cross the river, and he fought so bravely that Prataparudradeva fled in fear.

After this provisional victory against his sworn enemy, Krishnadevaraya returned to Kondavidu to take the all-important fort. One historian claimed the fort, situated on the summit of a craggy hill range, had 'baffled all invaders' for centuries. Like Udayagiri it was high up, secure and well provisioned. And now that all entrances, roads and escape routes had been totally blockaded, Vijayanagara forces simply needed to wait for the fort inhabitants to eventually surrender out of starvation. But fresh from battle, Krishnadevaraya was impatient and eager to exact a blow upon his retreating foe's territories. As Nunes states, Kondavidu had 'not yet experienced the king's strength' and so Krishnadevaraya redoubled his efforts and ordered a full-scale assault. With Timmarasu at the fore, the Vijayanagara troops were quick to take the offensive. Although evidence of this attack is scanty, an inscription from the Ahobilam temple offers some interesting details about Krishnadevaraya's siege tactics: the troops 'surrounded the fort and erected moveable wooden platforms to stand level with the defenders. They demolished the outer walls, scaled up on all sides to capture the fort.' And so in less than three months, Kondavidu fort capitulated in late June of 1515.

Inside the fort were several Gajapati nobles and

relatives including Prataparudradeva's wife, the Gajapati queen, and his son, Prince Virabhadra. One can imagine the motley crew of nobles, huddled and hungry within their high hill fortress with the armies of Krishnadevaraya knocking down their walls. But the king was noble of heart – he treated all the prisoners with respect and sent many of them (including Prince Virabhadra) back to Vijayanagara as royal guests. As the king recorded in verse: 'The hilltop fortresses of Kondavidu and Udayagiri, like ornaments upon the earth, were taken by my powerful arms. I spared the life of Virabhadra, the Gajapati's son, and captured all his relatives alive.'

The responsibility of administering the fort and its surrounding areas was given to Timmarasu, who entrusted it to his nephew Nadindla Gopa. Timmarasu continued the march north, towards the auxiliary fortress of Kondapalli, which was the last standing obstacle to Vijayanagara sovereignty in Andhra country. At this juncture, Krishnadevaraya returned home for a short stay, stopping once again at Tirupati and visiting other pilgrimage centres like Ahobilam and Srisailam on his way back to Vijayanagara.

At the capital, Krishnadevaraya called upon Prince Virabhadra personally. 'People had said that he was a very active man, and very dexterous with both sword and dagger.' The king was keen to see him fence and called on him along with one of his own expert swordsmen so they might spar. But when Virabhadra arrived, he was offended with the king for sending a man of humble birth, and not the son of a king, to fight against him. He cried out to the king, 'God forbid that I should soil my hands by touching a man not of royal blood!' And with these words he killed himself. Prataparudradeva, hearing of his son's sad demise, and fearing for his queen's safety, wrote to Timmarasu asking by what ransom he might regain his captive wife from the uncivilized king of Vijayanagara. This episode highlights an ongoing theme that would continue to be an issue for Krishnadevaraya throughout his life. Unlike the kshatriya Prataparudradeva, Krishnadevaraya came from humble stock, he was the son of a shudra general and a low-caste mother, a dasi-putra as the Gajapati often called him. The unfortunate incident of Prince Virabhadra's death only inflamed the seething personal enmity between the two kings. For now Prataparudradeva was at a disadvantage and Krishnadevaraya was set to force his hand.

Some eighty kilometres northeast of Kondavidu lay the fortress of Kondapalli on the north bank of the Krishna river in the middle of a dense forest. It was the last stronghold of Gajapati power in the Andhra region, and Krishnadevaraya was anxious to claim it for himself. The king had left instructions for Timmarasu to secure the surrounding areas and push north to Kondapalli where several of Prataparudradeva's relatives and officers had hunkered down as a last refuge. Some of these Gajapati loyalists had likely fled the fort at Kondavidu, which, according to legend, was designed with a secret escape route by its former Reddy stewards. Krishnadevaraya played with this notion as he composed an amusing historical verse:

> Krishnaraya, greatest of kings, this is amazing!
> As you lead a campaign to reclaim your lands,
> all the defeated lords and warriors of Kalinga,
> though their bodies were mangled,
> sought to reach the maidens of heaven!
> It seems the fort's former masters
> built some secret passageway
> from the city of Kondavidu
> directly to Lord Indra's heavenly capital!

Kondapalli, the last remnant of the Gajapati's southern administration, was on the brink of surrender. As Timmarasu marched north, his forces relentlessly subjugated the fort's neighbouring lands, taking Vijayawada and 'ravaging all the country which had no reason for expecting him'. The *Rayavacakamu* reports that 'the vanguard of his army forced its way into the outlying hamlets and wrought havoc by raping and ransacking everything in sight'. Finally, in the autumn of 1515, the army reached the southern bank of the Krishna river. And it was here that Krishnadevaraya likely rejoined his main forces and prepared for the final attack on Kondapalli.

With a huge restocked force, Krishnadevaraya and his men crossed the mighty Krishna in order to attack the fort. Their siege pressed hard and the fortress of Kondapalli surrendered after five months of stiff resistance. Krishnadevaraya's own memory of this victory reads with much more vitality:

> The minister Prahareshvara and others
>   were in the fort of Kondapalli,
> armed with strategic weaponry that touched the sky,
>   and protected by a battalion of Orissan soldiers.
> But with a sword in my hand like a snake,
>   I brilliantly seized the fort after an intense effort!

Even when the Gajapati dispatched a force in defence of the fort, it was easily repelled by one of Krishnadevaraya's contingent battalions. And so, in the winter of 1515, fell the last Gajapati fort in Andhra. According to the *Rayavacakamu*, the king's forces destroyed the fort and went on to sow every inch of ground in the surrounding hamlets with prickly weeds.

This harsh and uncharacteristically extreme treatment of the land suggests that Krishnadevaraya wanted not only to conquer the Gajapati, but to crush and humiliate him in the eyes of his subjects.

There seems to be some discrepancy about who was sheltered inside the fort of Kondapalli. The presence of a Gajapati prince and queen seems to have been confounded with accounts of the fall of Kondavidu. Whatever the case may be, the fort at Kondapalli housed some of Prataparudradeva's most senior lords including the Gajapati minister Praharesvara Patra and a Muslim nobleman named Bijili Khan. Also inside the fort was a large group of royal women which included some high-ranking queens. Here is Peddana's imaginative rendering of how women fleeing the Vijayanagara onslaught might have felt: 'The innocent young women of the Gajapati's harem, seeking refuge in the caves of the Vindhyas, looked out with wonder to a strange red darkness approaching them, as Krishnaraya's invading army kicked up a cloud of dusty red earth!' Luckily those who remained in the fort were treated honourably, for Krishnadevaraya pardoned all his captives and offered them every courtesy due to their royal personage. A verse from the king's political maxims was probably written with this moment in mind: 'Conquer enemy territories by taking control of their forts, but when you seize the harem, treat the women with respect, and in the custom of their native land. Never use harsh language with their ambassadors, for there may come a time for reconciliation.' The women were indeed treated well, but the time for peace had not yet arrived.

After Kondapalli, Krishnadevaraya's impressive chain of victories did not end. All the smaller fortresses in the surrounding areas fell like a row of toppling dominoes. And so, by the end of 1515, Prataparudradeva had lost all his territory south of the river Krishna, the traditional dividing line between the two great empires. Krishnadevaraya had brilliantly reconquered all the land he claimed was rightfully his, but he wasn't satisfied. His growing ego, along with a personal desire to humiliate his bitter rival, drove him on. Krishnadevaraya was bent on publicly defeating Prataparudradeva in open combat, and so, against the sage advice of Timmarasu, the eager young king pushed further north, straight into the heart of Gajapati country.

9

Rival Kings

When the king set out to the north in pursuit of Prataparudradeva, he left Timmarasu in command of Kondavidu to protect his rear and western flanks. There were still many potential dangers about as the Gajapati continued to be 'master of the eastern half of Telangana'. A major threat came from one Citap Khan, who was in charge of Warangal, Khammam and the surrounding areas. He was a Muslim chief, and like Bijili Khan who was earlier found in Kondapalli fort, Citap Khan was either a subordinate of the Gajapati, or a strongman dispatched by the Qutb Shahi sultan of Golconda. One account describes him as a recent convert to Islam; apparently he 'vanquished Muslims and wrested from them the beautiful city of Ekasilapuri (Warangal)' before taking on his new identity. If Citap Khan was indeed a vassal of the Qutb

Shah, it evidences how a Muslim sultan had banded together with a Hindu king in order to defeat another Hindu king. But whatever his affiliations, a character like Citap Khan typifies the fluidity of Deccani identity politics. Allegiances cut across religious, linguistic and ethnic lines; they were practical measures born of necessity rather than communal loyalties.

In 1512, two years into Krishnadevaraya's reign, the sultan Quli Qutb-ul-Mulk declared independence from the Bahmanis and went on to establish his own Golconda sultanate. He secured his dominion in the Telangana region with the help of Citap Khan and other local rulers who were ready and willing to forge new political ties. And although the Qutb Shahi never engaged with Krishnadevaraya in direct battle, it seems probable that he discharged Citap Khan to harass this powerful new threat on the borders of his realm. Timmarasu was reported to have a force of 2,00,000 men, and with 'very little fear' they engaged Citap Khan and routed his forces. In addition they took many spoils from the battle including horses, elephants, much money and stores of jewels. And so with his newly reclaimed territories secure behind him, Krishnadevaraya marched forward to engage with his arch-nemesis face to face.

Krishnadevaraya and Prataparudradeva were outwardly very alike because they both endeavoured, in their own ways, to embody the ideals of a righteous Hindu king. The ancient Indian conception of kingship was rooted in the mutually legitimizing relationship between brahmans and kshatriyas – the embodied representatives of knowledge and power, religion and politics. With flowery poems of praise, brahmans promoted a king's divine image, and in turn, kings would patronize brahman poets by gifting them both land and wealth. This symbiotic bond effectively consolidated power, both spiritual and political, in the hands of the two upper varnas. Krishnadevaraya and Prataparudradeva both played the part of the devout king who generously supported brahmans, but there was one major difference between the two, something that would underlie the intense animosity each held for the other.

Unlike the royal-blooded Prataparudradeva of the Solar Lineage, Krishnadevaraya was by all accounts a shudra, the unplanned offspring of a low-caste general and a *dasi* (servant woman). One story tells of an auspicious falling star that flashed across the sky at the moment of Krishnadevaraya's conception. On that night his father Narasa Nayaka lay with a maidservant who had come to light the evening lamps. According to Narayana Rao, 'In his own locality, Krishnadevaraya was only a peasant and, if legends are to be believed, a low-caste peasant at that.' According to oral tradition, Prataparudradeva looked down at Krishnadevaraya with contempt. He felt it below his high stature to engage with a son of a servant, a low-class upstart with no social standing. Prataparudradeva only saw Krishnadevaraya as a dasi-putra who had grafted himself on to the royal Lunar Lineage. Clearly, this was a major point of tension, but Krishnadevaraya seems to have made every effort to live up to the ideal of a righteous Hindu king, regardless of (or perhaps because of) his humble origins.

In their personal devotions, Krishnadevaraya and Prataparudradeva were both staunch Vaishnavas. At the same time, they were inclusive and tolerant in supporting state patronage of various other deities, sects and religious movements. And although both kings worshipped the main god Vishnu, they supported two separate traditions of Vaishnava theology: Krishnadevaraya was a Sri Vaishnava, a follower of the Tamil saint Ramanuja, while Prataparudradeva was an ardent Gaudiya, having converted to this new faith after a profound encounter with its celebrated founder, the Bengali saint Chaitanya Mahaprabhu.

One way to better understand the publicly perceived identities of both kings is to look closely at the royal epithets that commemorated them. Brahman court pandits eulogized their patron kings in hyperbolic terms, often deploying vapid stock phrases that reappeared generation after generation, like the hackneyed *rajadhiraja* or 'King of kings!' At other times the poets used specific, historically rooted language, like Krishnadevaraya being the 'King of Karnataka' or Prataparudradeva being the 'King of Kalinga'. In both cases, the king was being praised, even worshipped, as a god on earth, a bodily manifestation of righteous governance and dharma in action. Prataparudradeva, for example, was believed to be an 'avatara of Jagannatha', while Krishnadevaraya's court pandits declared that he was 'a living Krishna'. This process by which the king took on divine status had been evolving for centuries, and perhaps the clearest indication of this change was the insertion of the term *deva* or god into the names of these kings. During Krishnadevaraya's own time he was known only as Krishnaraya, and the addition of 'deva' seems to have happened much after his death, probably in the seventeenth century by when much of the 'golden age' history of Vijayanagara had crystallized.

Krishnadevaraya's imminent victory over the Gajapati would garner him the title *gajapati-gajakuta-pakala*, 'a fever upon the Gajapati's troops of elephants'. Sadly, however, 'almost all sources from Orissa are curiously silent' about Krishnadevaraya. Perhaps this is proof of the adage that only winners write history. In that sense both kings memorialized their victories over their Muslim neighbours. Prataparudradeva was called *hussain shahi suratrana sharana-rakshaka*, for giving protection to

Sultan Hussain Shah who 'threw himself on his mercy', while Krishnadevaraya was given the title *yavana-rajya-sthapanacarya*, or the Establisher of Yavana Rule, after he re-enthroned a disenfranchised Bahmani sultan.

The brahman eulogizers at court were masters of languages and poetry; they brought kings to life and committed their memory to the palm leaves of history. But Krishnadevaraya and Prataparudradeva were both well educated; they were scholars and accomplished poets in their own right and actively participated in the creation of their literary legacies. Indeed, this was very much in line with another important theme of Indian kingship: the ideal of a *kavi-raja* or poet-king. As Sanskrit scholar Sheldon Pollock notes, the figure of the learned ruler 'became virtually mandatory for the fully realized form of kingliness'. To be a truly righteous Hindu monarch, one had to be a master of both body and mind – a monarch and a philosopher who could rule with both might and wisdom. The most famous Indian example of such an enlightened monarch is Bhoja, the legendary philosopher-king who ruled half a millennium earlier in the Malwa country. The tales surrounding King Bhoja and his court of culture seem to have set the standard for the model kavi-raja, and so it is not surprising that Krishnadevaraya was commonly known as *abhinava-bhoja*, 'a New Bhoja,' *sakala-kala-bhoja*, 'Bhoja in all arts,' and simply Andhra Bhoja.

Central to this ancient belief was the balance between a king's body and his mind. He was to be a mighty warrior, of course, but also a man of culture and scholarly wisdom. A kavi-raja had mastery of *śastra* (weapons) and *śāstra* (texts), and so he was equipped to rule a vast kingdom with both strength and compassion. As the court pandits in Vijayanagara declared of Krishnadevaraya: 'You are an emperor in the fields of war and letters!' The Gajapati was eulogized in a similar vein as 'Lord of ninety million citizens, conversant in music and literature'. Below the surface of these grand epithets, however, the differences between these kings was striking.

Prataparudradeva was a high-born kshatriya writing in classical Sanskrit, while Krishnadevaraya was a low-caste shudra writing in a vernacular. And although they were both steeped in a great Sanskrit literary tradition, their poetic productions were starkly different. Prataparudra's major composition was the *Sarasvati Vilasam*, a Sanskrit work on *dharmashastra* that 'embraced the entire range of the religious, moral and civil laws of the Hindus'. Rather than an original contribution, however, it was more of a compilation of previous writers with no new opinions or insights. Furthermore, many literary scholars believe that the text wasn't even written by the king, but by his court poet Lolla Lakshmidhara Pandita. In contrast, Krishnadevaraya produced one of the most important and original texts of Telugu literature. His *Amuktamalyada* which tells the story of the Tamil poet-saint Andal is both fresh and exciting. As Narayana Rao and Shulman observe, 'This remarkable book is couched in a unique style . . . an enormous erudition in many branches of traditional science and learning is brought to bear upon scenes of ordinary life. Both an extraordinary realism and a sweeping imagination come into play . . . this highly crafted style was beyond imitation; no later Telugu poets attempted anything like it.' In addition, the *raja niti* section of *Amuktamalyada* is a truly unique contribution to Indian political theory; unlike the *Sarasvati Vilasam*, it expanded on older concepts and integrated a lived knowledge of sixteenth-century governance.

For Prataparudradeva, scholasticism and erudition were an inheritance – his father Purushottama was a highly accomplished scholar with many literary works to his credit. Krishnadevaraya could claim no such ancestral right. He had to work for it, and he surely did. These fundamental differences between Krishnadevaraya and Prataparudradeva undergirded the long conflict and personal enmity between the two kings. Now after a long campaign that had already lasted for over three years, Krishnadevaraya pressed into Gajapati territory, north along the coast towards the famed temple of Simhachalam.

10

The Lion Mountain

Located just fifteen kilometres north of the bustling present-day port city of Visakhapatnam on the Bay of Bengal, the stunning Varaha Lakshmi Narasimha temple rises from a verdant hill known as Simhachalam, the Lion Mountain. According to temple legends, this was the hill that the demon Hiranyakashipu used to crush his son Prahlada, one of many failed attempts to kill the boy who was an ardent devotee of Vishnu. Later the pious Prahlada established this temple to honour Vishnu's avataras as Varaha the boar and Narasimha the man-lion. This hybrid avatara is supposed to have a boar's head, a human torso and a lion's tail, but curiously, the temple's central idol is a simple stone, so charged with spiritual energy that it must be covered in layer upon layer of cooling sandalwood paste.

Historically, the temple seems to have been active from at least the ninth century, receiving steady patronage from several dynasties including the Chalukyas, Eastern Gangas, Reddys, Gajapatis and Vijayanagara. Then, just as today, pilgrims from Andhra, Orissa and other areas flocked to the temple, especially on the day of Akshaya Tritiya, the one special day of the year when the golden-brown sandalwood paste is removed from the stone idol. For Krishnadevaraya this important spiritual centre would now serve as a base for the final push of his Gajapati campaign. Krishnadevaraya's arrival at Simhachalam in mid-1516 occasioned many generous gifts to Lord Narasimha. Temple inscriptions record that the king gifted (in honour of his parents) a pearl necklace, a pair of diamond-studded bracelets, a golden plate and heaps of gold coins. In addition, his accompanying queens Chinnadevi and Tirumaladevi each gifted a pendant and 500 gold coins to the main deity. And like his many pilgrimages to Tirupati, his lavish gifts expressed his deep devotion and prayers of victory.

With his mighty army camped at Potnuru, some forty kilometres north of Simhachalam and squarely located in Gajapati territory, Krishnadevaraya anxiously awaited Prataparudradeva's advance. He sent taunting messages saying, 'I'm waiting for you on the battlefield!' but the Gajapati gave no reply. And although Krishnadevaraya had the means to order a full-scale attack, he wanted his enemy to come to him. It was this moment that likely prompted the composition of a rather poetic political verse: 'Like a fisherman on a riverbank, who slowly pulls on his rope to haul in a big fish pierced with a barbed spear, a king should not capture a strong enemy when he is afraid, he should rather let him come slowly of his own accord.'

But even after six long months of waiting, Prataparudradeva was nowhere to be seen. And although he may have indeed been fearful of Krishnadevaraya's forces, his absence in the south was probably due to the fact that he was busy defending his northern frontier from incursions led by Hussain Shah, the sultan of Bengal. Be that as it may, Krishnadevaraya's patience was exhausted. His adversary's cowardly unwillingness to engage in battle turned the king's frustration to fury.

According to Nunes, Krishnadevaraya 'did many works' in and around Potnuru. He erected 'a very grand temple to which he gave much revenue. And he commanded to engrave on it an inscription which read, "Perhaps when these letters are worn away, the king of Orissa will give battle to the king of Vijayanagara. If the king of Orissa ignores us, his queen shall be given over to the smiths who shoe the horses of Vijayanagara!"' It seems odd that such harsh language would be inscribed on a temple wall. In fact we have no other evidence of this temple's existence, nor any corroborating information regarding the inscription. In all likelihood, the story is an embellishment of Krishnadevaraya's installation of a *jaya-stambha* (victory pillar) in Potnuru. Several sources make mention of this event, and even some locals in Potnuru today claim that a darkened rock in the centre of town is a remnant of the famous pillar. Perhaps the best memorialization of the incident comes from Krishnadevaraya himself who writes: 'In Simhachalam I gained merit by making ritual offerings of great devotion to the feet of the Lord of the Illusionary Lion. I erected a victory pillar in Potnuru, a monolithic memorial engraved with the eight syllables of my name – the blessed King Krishnaraya!' Koteswara Rao believes that these eight syllables are *śrī-kṛṣṇarāya-nṛpati*, or Sri Krishnaraya Lord of Men, a simple but apt declaration of his supremacy over the Gajapatis.

Krishnadevaraya was anxious to press north in pursuit of Prataparudradeva, but his astute minister advised caution. Timmarasu knew that the Gajapati was surrounded by his sixteen *mahapatras* or great vassals. This loyal force was believed to be invincible, and Timmarasu realized that he would have to destabilize them before launching a full-scale attack. As a well-versed scholar in his own right, Timmarasu turned to the classical political theory of Kautilya as enumerated in his magnum opus, the *Arthashastra.* In this ancient text on state governance, four *upayas* or stratagems are prescribed for dealing with enemy kings: *sama* (conciliation), *dana* (gift giving), *danda* (attack) and *bheda* (dissension). By Timmarasu's reckoning, their only viable option now was bheda: to provoke discord among the mahapatras and thereby weaken Prataparudradeva's support structure. He explained to Krishnadevaraya that 'sowing dissension in the enemy's camp is the best expedient for a desperate king. It can lead a king to safety from even the worst perils! But . . . it will be at the expense of vast quantities of priceless jewels.'

Although the following episode may be fictitious, it has entered popular folk memory as evidence of Timmarasu's shrewd political mind. As the story goes, Timmarasu had sixteen treasure chests filled with gold and fine jewels to gift to each of the mahapatras. Every chest also contained a letter that thanked the mahapatra for his aid to Vijayanagara, and promised him further rewards after the successful capture of Prataparudradeva's capital of Cuttack. Next, Timmarasu's men conspicuously carried the chests straight into Gajapati territory, and just as Timmarasu had planned, they were duly captured and brought before Prataparudradeva. Seeing the treasure-laden chests and reading the letters inside, the Gajapati flew into a rage. He was shocked and infuriated by this blatant betrayal, but he grew fearful for his life and fled. Some say he escaped under the cover of darkness to avoid any confrontation with his traitorous lords.

At this point the historical record becomes somewhat hazy. Although there is no concrete evidence of Krishnadevaraya's attack on Cuttack, it seems to have occurred sometime in 1518. A popular Telugu folk song hints at the king's advance to the Gajapati capital: 'Warangal is ours! Kondapalli is ours! If you dare dispute it, even Cuttack is ours!' The Gajapati capital was situated on a thin strip of land that extends into the Mahanadi river delta, almost like an island fortress. It was from here that Prataparudradeva ran to the hills in fear. Here is how Krishnadevaraya, in one highly stylized Telugu verse, imagined his rival's cowardly flight:

> The Gajapati disguised himself as a cowherd
>   and fled to the Vindhyas.
> And there in a dark cave, he hid in fear
>   and spent the night in a restless sleep.
> When he awoke, a snake skin caught in his hair
>   appeared like a battle helmet,
> while a peacock feather clinging to his head
>   sparkled like a tricolored tassel.
> His body was covered in cobwebs
>   like a finely woven robe, and as he stepped

out of the cave, his brow scraped a rock,
    giving him a tilakam of blood and dirt.
Then in a mountain pool he saw his reflection,
    and thought that by some magic
in those hills, his disguise had transformed
    back to his former royal attire!

According to Nunes's description of the siege of Catuir, a city that in many ways fits the description of Cuttack, we learn of Krishnadevaraya's unique strategy in capturing the island-like fortresses. First the king made ready a large army and laid siege to the city. But the river surrounding the city had swollen and was flowing with so much water that he could do nothing. Anxious for victory, he commanded his men to dig fifty wide troughs all around the river. This was done in short time since he had so many soldiers. Next they dug channels to connect the troughs to the river, and all the water quickly flowed out. Now the river was so shallow you could see the bottom, and Krishnadevaraya and his men easily reached the city gates.

Nunes reports that inside the fort-city were 1,00,000 foot soldiers with 3,000 horses 'who defended themselves and fought very bravely. But this did little to prevent Krishnadevaraya from entering in a few days and slaughtering them all.' In line with the king's political philosophy, however, he was much kinder to the city's general populace and granted 'amnesty to its inhabitants and help to those who wanted to leave'. When the Vijayanagara troops stormed the palace they found many treasures inside, including 16,00,000 *pardaos* (gold coins), loads of jewels, numerous horses and some elephants. And when the seizure was complete, Krishnadevaraya divided the loot among his many captains, carefully giving each his just due. The judicious sharing of victory spoils was yet another practice that instilled loyalty in his men who had endured a long and often arduous campaign.

Krishnadevaraya's sack of Cuttack was so total, so heavy that the Gajapati empire would never recover. Prataparudradeva eventually sued for peace in order to save his country from further devastation. And upon this final victory, Krishnadevaraya made his intentions clear: 'I want you to realize that I have come solely for the sake of increasing my glory, with no desire of annexing your kingdom. The Gajapati kingdom I leave for the Gajapati.'

By all accounts a peace treaty was negotiated in August 1519, three years after Krishnadevaraya first arrived in Simhachalam. After such a bitter build-up, the king was now rather conciliatory. The long-accepted line of demarcation between the two empires was the mighty Krishna river, and so all the lands north of the river, including the cities of Cuttack and Kondapalli, were restored to Prataparudradeva. From Krishnadevaraya's point of view, he was realizing Saluva Narasimha's dream by restoring the Vijayanagara empire to its past glory. At this point, Krishnadevaraya was less interested in expanding the empire's borders and more concerned with re-establishing what he believed to be his kingdom's sovereign dominion. More importantly, he seems to have wanted to shame Prataparudradeva, forcing him to concede defeat and publicly accept Krishnadevaraya as a worthy Hindu king. As the king reportedly said to his rival, 'After all, is there any real difference between you and me?' The *Rayavacakamu* would make it seem that Krishnadevaraya was asserting they were both Hindus, but what he was really saying was that they were both of equal social status.

Like many royal accords throughout history, the new peace between Vijayanagara and the Gajapatis was sealed with a handsome dowry and a contrived marriage. After Krishnadevaraya honourably freed the Gajapati queen, Prataparudradeva offered the king his daughter in marriage. Numerous tales surround this new queen of Vijayanagara. She is known variously as Kamala, Lakshmi, Jaganmohini, Bhadra and Tukka, but most often as Annapurna. Nunes describes one version of how the alliance was finally effected: Prataparudradeva 'sent ambassadors to Vijayanagara to arrange a marriage with his daughter, with which Krishnadevaraya was well content; and when the king of Orissa knew his will, he sent him his daughter; and with her coming the two enemies became friends. Krishnadevaraya restored the lands on the other side of the river, and kept those on this side for himself.'

This rosy picture contrasts with most folk legends which focus on Annapurna's poor treatment at the Vijayanagara court. One tradition, vividly depicted in the 1962 Telugu film *Mahamantri Timmarasu*, maintains that Annapurna feigned true love for the king only so she could avenge her father's defeat. As Subrahmanyam records, 'A tradition prevails that the Gajapati princess, at the instigation of her father, made an attempt on Krishnadevaraya's life; but that catastrophe was averted by the sagacity and tact of his minister Timmarasu.' After this failed assassination attempt, Krishnadevaraya is said to have completely neglected his new queen. She in turn opened old wounds by calling him a dasi-putra, unfit to marry a woman of noble birth like herself. Krishnadevaraya could not tolerate the insult and had Annapurna exiled to Kambham, where she would live out her days in poverty and solitude. Other legends claim that Prataparudradeva had money and expensive jewels sent to his exiled and destitute daughter, but Annapurna seems to have turned to a life of charity. Locals in Kambham still claim that Annapurna sold all her jewels to sponsor the construction of a large water reservoir.

We will probably never know the truth about this sordid marriage alliance. For Prataparudradeva, this ignominious surrender was the beginning of the end for his celebrated dynasty. The power vacuum created in the eastern Deccan would soon be filled by the expanding Qutb Shahi sultanate of Golconda. And all vestiges of Gajapati power would finally disappear just a year after Prataparudradeva's death in 1540. Ironically, Krishnadevaraya's sworn enemy would outlive him; one tradition maintains that Prataparudradeva, still sore from the humiliating defeat, determined to attack Vijayanagara immediately upon Krishnadevaraya's death in 1529. Allasani Peddana, the Vijayanagara poet laureate, 'rebuked him for his impudence' by composing a verse recounting the Gajapati's many losses at the hands of the king. As the story goes, when the verse was relayed to Prataparudradeva, he backed down out of shame and fear.

The verse mentioned in this tale could very well be a praise poem from Peddana's masterpiece, the *Manu Caritramu*. With one propulsive and fiery string of vivid descriptors, Peddana dramatically recounts each of Krishnadevaraya's victories from the long-fought Gajapati campaign. And though the effusive tone of Telugu court poetry is often hyperbolic, perhaps in this case Peddana struck the right tone in summarizing the king's brilliant military exploits.

> In the very beginning, a blazing bright fire was sparked
> when the king's steel sword struck the flint of Udayagiri.
> The flames rose towards Kondavidu where Lord Kasavapatra
> was torched like tinder. The blaze spread quickly,
> raging through the Jammi Valley, scorching Kona
> and striking Kottam. The glow of golden Kanakagiri
> turned to black, and the waters of the Godavari boiled!
> Potnuru burned, Mademulu roasted, and Oddadi
> was left in smolders! And while Cuttack burned,
> the Gajapati fled in fear of the devastating trail of fires
> set ablaze by Krishnaraya's mighty arms!

Finally, in late 1519, Krishnadevaraya triumphantly marched back to Vijayanagara and never again returned to Orissa. His ever-watchful minister Timmarasu stayed in the area south of the Krishna and oversaw issues of governance and matters of dispute, including a brief but divisive victory over Golconda forces. As Nunes recounts, when Timmarasu eventually returned to Vijayanagara, he was received by the king as 'the principal person in the kingdom'. And so with king and minister back in the capital, a period of relative peace and stability would be enjoyed by all. After over six years of constant battle away from home, the long Orissa campaign was behind him, and Krishnadevaraya was ready to enjoy the pleasures of his palace.

Part III

11

Court of Culture

By 1520, a decade into Krishnadevaraya's reign, Vijayanagara was famed beyond its borders as a cosmopolitan metropolis, a sprawling city expansive in both size and spirit. The capital was truly a place of diversity and inclusion where people of varying faiths, ethnicities and classes would not only intermingle but also cooperate in building what Paes called 'the best provided city in the world . . . large as Rome, and very beautiful to the sight'. He went on to add that 'in this city you will find men belonging to every nation and people . . . countless in number, so much so that I do not wish to write it down for fear it should be thought fabulous'. Or as Duarte Barbosa writes in one of the first examples of Portuguese travel literature: 'There is an endless number of merchants, wealthy men and natives of the city to whom the king allows such freedom that every man may come and go and live according to his own creed . . . great equity and justice is observed to all, not only by the rulers, but by the people one to another.' Indeed, much of this cosmopolitan ethos was fuelled by international traders who brought goods and ideas from all around the world to the bustling south Indian city.

The image of the multicultural city was propagated throughout the subcontinent by court poets who eulogized kings and commemorated their victories. It was the poets of Vijayanagara who truly sang the empire into the people's imagination and the pages of history. As the *Rayavacakamu* records: The king spent the day at court 'with a full assembly of scholars, poets, and palace officers skilled at telling pleasant stories . . . they all looked at Krishnadevaraya and said, "Just as the fame and glory of the kings who ruled long ago are preserved in the literary works they commissioned, you too should commission works so that your fame and glory will endure forever."'

The epicentre of Vijayanagara literary production was a great hall called the Bhuvana Vijayam, or World Conquest, designed to host poetry readings and contests of literary wit. According to Paes, the hall was built when the king returned from the war against Orissa. It was a wide open space with lofty walls covered from top to bottom with crimson and green velvet and other handsome cloths.

The magnificent structure was metaphorically held up by the king's *ashta-dig-gajas*, or Elephants of the Eight Directions, great poets of the land whom Krishnadevaraya had invited to grace his court. In Hindu cosmology, the mythical eight elephants support the entire universe on their backs, and so it was only fitting for the king to bestow this lofty title upon the celebrated poets who sustained the empire by memorializing the king's fame. To be sure, there was a deep and sustained connection between political power and literary production. The king's royal poets not only crafted words, but they also helped shape whole empires.

The king's poet laureate and close confidant was Allasani Peddana. He was perhaps the most celebrated Telugu poet of his time; Krishnadevaraya even named him the grandsire of Telugu poetry. In one verse from his famed *Manu Caritramu*, Peddana vividly describes the ambience within the Bhuvana Vijayam, where women with eyes like blue sapphires and faces radiant as the moon fanned the king with yak-tail fans while he joyously sat on the throne in the company of learned people. Scholars discussed the fine points of Paninian grammar, Kanada's atomistic philosophy, Badarayana's metaphysics and more. But Krishnadevaraya was not a mere spectator during such affairs; his prodigious scholarship and literary acumen allowed him not only to oversee but actively engage in philosophical debates and literary discussions. He was creating a court of culture, and a culture for court, by surrounding himself with the finest scholars and poets of the land, and positioning himself at the very centre of it all.

Although the kings of Vijayanagara were inclusive in their patronage of various literatures, including Sanskrit, Tamil and Kannada, the reign of Krishnadevaraya witnessed the ascendancy of Telugu as the pre-eminent language of the empire. We know Krishnadevaraya patronized poets in other languages, like Hariharadasa in Tamil and Lolla Lakshmidhara in Sanskrit, but this was Telugu's moment – it was a language of the people. All of the famed poets of the Vijayanagara octet wrote in Telugu, though not exclusively. Most poets then, as the case remains in India even today, were multilingual speakers as well as writers. In addition to expertise in two or three regional languages, any poet worth his salt would be proficient in Sanskrit – it was the sine qua non of scholastic merit and poetic authority. That being said, vernacular literatures were receiving more and more patronage from local kings, and although Sanskrit remained a language of prestige, regional languages now dominated the realm of lyrical poetry. And so it was that Krishnadevaraya presided over not only a vast earthly empire but a vibrant literary one as well. No wonder his court poets cried, 'O mighty lord, king of kings, supreme sovereign of heroic splendor! You are united like the Highest God – half the goddess Durga, half the Lord of Dance – an emperor in the fields of war and letters!'

In addition to the daily goings-on at the Bhuvana Vijayam, the Vasantotsavam, or annual Spring Festival, was a favourite occasion to gather poets for a celebration. As Timmana writes in his *Parijata Apaharanamu*: 'Every year during the Spring Festival, an enthusiastic crowd of great poets would arrive with their finely crafted poems. Just the thought of it excited the women of the palace, but the king calmed them all down with his charm.' Like the legendary King Bhoja before him, Krishnadevaraya delighted in celebrating the annual Spring Festival when aspiring poets from far and wide would arrive at the court for a series of literary events, debates and competitions in which the king bestowed gifts of gold on the most skilled poets. It was at one such festival that the king premiered his Sanskrit play entitled *Jambavati Kalyanam*. A temple inscription tells us the 'drama was enacted before the people assembled to witness the Chaitra Spring festival'. In this way, literature in premodern India was more than a means of entertainment – it functioned as a communal spectacle that celebrated the power and culture of the empire and its king. It would be no exaggeration to say that Krishnadevaraya of Vijayanagara was at the apex of a south Indian cultural renaissance. This was a vibrant period of vernacularization when old Sanskrit texts and traditions were being revived, translated and reformulated for new and broader audiences. Indeed, this remarkable age of cultural production witnessed innovations in everything from literature, music and dance to architecture, sculpture and painting.

Of the eight great poets who adorned the king's court, a few are noteworthy for their close connection to the king's life. First there was Allasani Peddana, the king's favourite poet. He composed the seminal *Manu Caritramu*, or Story of the First Man, a masterpiece of classical Telugu and a poetic manifesto for the empire. According to Peddana, Krishnadevaraya commissioned the great work knowing that it would outlast his reign, his empire and even his descendants. The king calls Peddana his friend, and oral tradition tells us they had a deep bond of mutual respect.

Another luminary of the Bhuvana Vijayam was Nandi Timmana, a Shaiva from an Andhra Niyogi Brahman family with roots in the Tamil country. According to tradition, Timmana was given as an *aranam* or wedding gift when Tirumaladevi was married to the king. And although he was a multilingual poet, Timmana's most celebrated work (which he dedicated to the king) was *Parijata Apaharanamu*, or Theft of Heaven's Tree, a stylized rendering of the Satyabhama story in Telugu. In it the poet describes how Krishna gives a precious parijata flower to his devout wife Rukmini. When his other wife Satyabhama finds out, she flies into a jealous rage and Krishna must appease her. She even kicks him, but he swears that he'll go all the way to heaven to bring her not only a flower, but the whole parijata tree. Timmana's chosen subject was no accident; in fact some say it was written expressively for the king as a lesson on how to deal with an upset queen. As per oral tradition, one night Krishnadevaraya woke up to find his queen Tirumaladevi turned around in bed with her feet touching his head. The king was aghast at the outrage and shunned her. In order to win back the king's affections, Tirumaladevi entreated her old friend Timmana to compose a great work that would change the king's heart. And so it was that the famous *Parijata Apaharanamu* came into existence. Here's an example of Timmana's clever language for Krishna's words to Satyabhama, or rather Krishnadevaraya's words to Tirumaladevi: 'Why are you sad, my lovely bride? All this just for a flower? I'm here for you. Listen, I'll go to Indra's garden. I don't even care if he tries to stop me. I'll bring back the whole parijata tree just for you!' And so in one single act, Timmana created a Telugu classic while fostering the conjugal bliss of the royal couple.

Another episode from this fabled story intersects with historical realities. The famous Tulapurusha rite was a public ceremony in which a king would weigh himself against a pile of gold and pearls and distribute the amassed wealth to learned brahmans. In the narrative, Satyabhama is tricked into a situation in which she has to give Krishna away as charity. The only way to reclaim him is to perform the rite and offer the people his weight in gold. But no matter how much of her great fortune she heaps on to the scale, nothing can outweigh Krishna. Finally, Rukmini offers a tiny branch from her tulsi plant, and the scales tip. This story, beautifully depicted in the classic 1966 Telugu film *Sri Krishna Tulabharam*, illustrates the power of bhakti, for a humble offering when given with true devotion becomes priceless. It is no coincidence then that Krishnadevaraya is known to have performed the Tulapurusha ceremony on multiple occasions; even today in the ruins of Hampi, one can see the great *tulabharam* (stone scale) on which the king might have weighed himself as a public spectacle.

Peddana's and Timmana's presence at the Vijayanagara court and their interactions with the king are well confirmed by the historical record. But one other poet is said to have been close to the king, even considered by some to be his most trusted personal adviser: the famous Tenali Ramakrishna. The historical poet Tenali Ramakrishna is often confounded with a popular figure from the oral tradition. His name was also Tenali Ramakrishna, and in Andhra he is remembered as the poet of wit – *vikatakavi*

వికటకవి – a charming palindrome when written in Telugu script. This Tenali fits into the well-known archetype of the witty court counsellor who is ever by the king's side à la Birbal and Akbar. Unfortunately, there is no historical evidence to suggest that such a person even existed, but the countless amusing stories that have built up around this lovable character contribute to how Krishnadevaraya and his court are remembered by people every day.

Those years after the Gajapati campaign were indeed a time of pleasure and repose, the court was bustling with scholars and poets, new construction projects were expanding the city limits, merchants from around the world came and went, and the city of Vijayanagara was truly at the height of its glory. After many years of battle, Krishnadevaraya finally had time to settle back into life at the capital. As Paes vividly describes, the king would wake before sunrise and massage his whole body with amber-coloured sesame oil before gulping down half a litre of the same. Wearing but a tiny loincloth he would exercise his arms by lifting great earthenware weights and practising with a sword until all the oil he had just consumed was sweated out of his body. Next he would spar with one of his wrestlers before mounting his horse and galloping over the plains until dawn. And then, after being bathed by a trusted brahman, he would go to his private temple to offer his daily prayers. Finally, he would make his way to the meeting hall where he would discuss matters of state with trusted officers and city governors.

The king adds to the lively picture with his own preferred schedule:

At dawn, before the physicians ask, 'Did you sleep well?'
    a king should consult his brahman astrologers.
After this, he should meet with his accountants
    to discuss state finances,
    before assembling his ministers and lords.
In the middle of the day,
    before training with wrestlers and masseuses
    a king should chat with cooks, farmers and hunters.
And as the day turns, he should honor venerable yogis
    and righteous men before worshipping the gods.
Then, after eating, a king should enjoy old stories told by poets
    before being entertained by his jester.
And in the evening he should be with dancers and singers,
    and in the night, with his lover, before a good night's rest.

It was a truly balanced day, filled with activities encompassing the range of religious, political, social and cultural aspects of court life. Clearly, the king enjoyed moving through various quarters of the palace and interacting with people of every station. For

Krishnadevaraya, culture was not only great poems or works of art, it was a way of being. *Yatha raja, tatha praja* goes the saying: as the king, so the subjects. And so, the single most important thing Krishnadevaraya did to promote the culture of his court was to embody within himself the exemplar of a cultured life.

12

Road to Raichur

After a few years of enjoying the pleasures of palace life, Krishnadevaraya's unsettled mind returned to the last words of his predecessor Saluva Narasimha. The forts of Mudgal and Udayagiri were now under Vijayanagara sovereignty, but Raichur, that prized and contested tract between the Krishna and Tungabhadra rivers, remained under the control of Bijapur. The final part of Saluva Narasimha's commandment had yet to be fulfilled and Krishnadevaraya was determined to make it so. But 'because there were many years of peace between both parties, he knew not how to break it'. But then Timmarasu reminded the king that the peace was brokered under certain conditions: 'If one side should harbour any land-owners, captains in revolt, or other evil-doers, the other side should hand them over forthwith.' In other words, there was an extradition clause built into the Vijayanagara–Bijapur peace treaty. Timmarasu continued, 'There was now great reason for breaking the peace, since many land-owners and debtors had fled into the kingdom of the Adil Shah. He counseled therefore that the king demand the surrender of these men, and should the Adil Shah refuse, there would be lawful grounds for the king to break the peace.' The majority of the king's councillors, however, disagreed with this advice.

With such advice in mind, Krishnadevaraya quietly dispatched a dependable officer named Cide Mercar with forty thousand pardaos to buy horses in Goa. This curious figure was a Muslim, very likely of African origin, and a trusted confidant of the king. And so following his master's command, Cide Mercar travelled to Ponda, near Portuguese-controlled Goa, under the pretext of securing horses from the Portuguese. There Cide Mercar seems to have 'fallen in' with some fellow Muslims, and thereafter conveniently absconded to Bijapur with all the money to seek asylum with the Adil Shah. When news of Cide Mercar's defection reached Krishnadevaraya back at the capital, the king promptly penned a friendly message to the Adil Shah, asking for the swift return of his man, and his money. The king waxed on about how nothing could shake their long friendship, and how he trusted that a traitor would not be the cause of breaking the peace between them. And so he called for Cide Mercar's immediate extradition.

At the Bijapuri court, the Adil Shah summoned his councillors and instructed them to read the letter in which 'many suggestions were made'. In the end, they unanimously agreed not to send Cide Mercar back, for they reckoned him 'one learned in the law and related to Muhammad'. The Adil Shah, 'as a cloak to his action', discharged Cide Mercar to the Bijapuri seaport of Dabul as a way of maintaining that he knew nothing of the traitor's whereabouts or intentions. Clearly, both Krishnadevaraya and the Adil Shah were posturing, playing at diplomatic skirmishes before what seemed like an imminent confrontation of arms.

When Krishnadevaraya's emissaries returned to Vijayanagara with the Adil Shah's response, the king was furious, and took it that the peace was broken. At once he called together the great lords of his council, and had the letter read out aloud so all might hear it. And as soon as it was read, he ordered them to make ready, since he was determined to take full vengeance. But the king's councillors advised against it, saying it was unwise to react to such a small issue, and that he should consider what would be said about him throughout the world. And that if he was bent on breaking the peace for such a trifling cause, 'he should call to mind that there never was any honesty in a Moor'. Clearly, the king's council had not grasped their commander's stratagem, nor had they understood the king's personal relationship with one particular Muslim, the double agent Cide Mercar.

The councillors could see that the king was determined to make war, so they advised him, 'Sire, do not go to war over Cide Mercar in Dabul, rather go against Raichur, which now belongs to the Adil Shah but of old was part of this kingdom. Then the Adil Shah will be forced to come to defend it, and there you can have your revenge!' The king agreed and prepared to set out. Krishnadevaraya sent letters to the other four Deccan sultans giving them an account of what had happened with the Adil Shah, and how he was determined to make war on him. The sultans replied that he was in the right, and that they would assist him as far as they were able. Krishnadevaraya was intent on making the Adil Shah's transgression a matter of public record; a political contract had been breached and war was the only remedy. The positive endorsement from the other Deccan sultans is yet another example of how political allegiances could transcend religious affiliations. As historical evidence bears out, the premodern Deccan was a complex arena of intersecting personal identities; it was only the relentless struggle for power that cut through them all.

And so it was that in early 1520 Krishnadevaraya

summoned his great armies to march upon the fort of Raichur in order to reclaim the coveted doab from the hands of the Adil Shah, and thereby make whole the sovereign empire of Vijayanagara. Mobilizing such a massive force must have taken weeks, if not months. Before Krishnadevaraya set out from the capital, an advance army, commanded by one Kama Nayaka, the king's trusted chief of guard, marched north with a force of sixteen elephants, 1,000 cavalry and 30,000 footmen made up of archers, shield bearers, spearmen and musketeers. Following some distance behind were the senior lords with their respective troops, led by high-ranking officers like Timmarasu, Kondamarasu and Ayyamarasu who each pledged tens of thousands of infantrymen, thousands of cavalrymen and hundreds of war elephants. Taking up the rear followed the king's three favourite eunuchs who could boast the charge of 40,000 foot, 1,000 horse and fifteen elephants. Even the king's faithful betel bearer could claim authority over 15,000 footmen and 200 horses. And last but not least, the king's personal guard which numbered some 40,000 archers and shield bearers and 6,000 horse, along with 300 of the finest elephants, because the king had his 'pick of all his kingdom'. At final count, the reckoning offered by Nunes puts Krishnadevaraya's army at well over half a million foot soldiers, almost 30,000 horses and over 500 elephants! No doubt an exaggeration, but Krishnadevaraya's title as the Narapati or Lord of Men was no empty moniker. The great southern empire of Vijayanagara was always able to muster unimaginably large numbers of fighting men, not to mention mighty herds of war elephants sourced from the realm's southern hills. As Aiyangar put it, 'Astoundingly large as the numbers appear it does not seem quite beyond the capacity of the empire of Krishnadevaraya to put this number into the field.' Whatever the actual numbers, the sight of such a vast army must have been truly beyond imagination.

What's more, these estimates were only in regard to soldiering men. The daily needs of such a force required the care and support of thousands of additional people. Great numbers of merchants with many supplies were sent out ahead of the army 'so wherever you may be, you will at once find all you want. Every captain has his merchants who are compelled to give him all the supplies needed for his people.' The men were thus well supplied on their relatively short fifty-league march to the fort of Raichur. And so with the Tungabhadra to his south and the Krishna river to his north, Krishnadevaraya and his massive army pitched their tents and made camp well beyond the range of the fort's gunmen.

As the war party set up camp, it was as if a whole

city, already well provisioned and bustling with activity, was rising up from the sandy riverbank. Nunes was overwhelmed by the sight. He remarked, 'I do not know who could describe it so as to be believed. It's a mystery how there should be such an abundance of everything out here!' There was the royal tent protected by 'a hedge of brush-wood and thorns' and nearby, where the king's personal priests stayed, were kept the sacred idols which the king honoured every day. Senior officers and eunuchs camped close by while a separate camp was made for scouts, and yet another one just for washermen. The main camp was well organized and partitioned by regular streets. Nunes records that 'each captain's division had its market, where you found all kinds of meat, such as sheep, goats, pigs, fowls, hares, partridges and other birds; so much so that it would seem as if you were in the city of Vijayanagara!' The camp's general market, stocked with corn and lentils, was a bazaar where you could 'find everything that you wanted in great abundance'. There were craftsmen of every kind, jewellers and cotton cloth sellers, washermen, women, scouts and water boys, not to mention hustling purveyors of grass and straw. As Nunes reminds us to do, just imagine the fodder required every single day 'for the consumption of thirty-two thousand four hundred horses and five hundred and fifty-one elephants, to say nothing of the sumpter-mules and asses, and the great numbers of oxen which carry all the supplies and many other burdens, such as tents and other things'. Finally he concludes that 'no one . . . would ever dream that a war was going on, but would think that he was in a prosperous city'.

The region's headquarter was the coveted stronghold of Raichur, positioned upon a conspicuous hill that rose like a woman's breast upon the earth. The city itself was surrounded by an impenetrable stone wall, built with three compact layers of heavy masonry. As historian Richard Eaton comments, 'With their massive slabs of finely dressed granite, these walls were, in their own day, considered an engineering marvel; even today, somc local residents regard them as the work of gods, not men.' The fort was also equipped with an imposing gate, an outer moat and several high and strong stone towers, erected so 'close together that one could hear words spoken from one to the other'. The citadel was no doubt well defended, almost impossible to take in a frontal assault, but it was also well provisioned, making the prospect of a siege appear hopeless. Atop the hill was said to be a mysterious spring which flowed with fresh water all year round. The locals thought it blessed, for even in their lofty position, they never wanted for water. The small garrison inside consisting of 8,000 foot, 400 horse and twenty elephants were confident they could survive a prolonged siege, even if it should last for five years! Krishnadevaraya's only way forward was to suffer the unavoidable loss of life that would accompany any attempt to penetrate the ramparts of Raichur.

Most threatening of all were the fort's catapults 'which hurled heavy stones and did great damage'. To boot, many well-armed artillerymen patrolled the walls at every hour, ever ready to fire upon would-be attackers. Nunes counted no less than 'two hundred pieces of heavy artillery, not to mention small ones'. Rifles, guns and cannons were not new to the subcontinent; they had slowly made their way into India even before the Europeans had, but according to Eaton, the battle of Raichur witnessed South Asia's 'earliest significant appearance of cannon – whether used offensively as field artillery, or used defensively on the battlements of forts – [and] the earliest known appearance of matchlock firearms'. Indeed, the imminent battle of Raichur would come to represent a 'transitional phase in the military history of South Asia' and a critical moment in the 'diplomatic history of the Deccan'. One reason for this unique distinction is that the 1520 battle of Raichur remains one of the most well-documented military engagements in premodern South Asian history. Much of the detailed information we have comes from Nunes, whose account of the battle reads like an eyewitness account. Reading the fine details makes one feel that Nunes must have been present for all the breathtaking action. The description that follows is largely taken from his chronicle.

Now that all of Krishnadevaraya's forces had assembled and everyone was on guard, the brahmans conducted their ceremonies and advised the king that the time was right to advance. Prayers, rituals and sacrifices were always a prelude to war, and following them came the great sound of war drums, trumpets and other instruments, all pounding into a thunderous intensity to rile up the anxious troops. Nunes found the din so terrific that he felt like heaven might come crashing down on him. The author of the *Rayavacakamu* echoes the sentiment:

With an impetuous thirst for conquest,
the lord of the world sounded the drums,
striking terror into the hearts of his foes.

As the drums' roar convulses the earth,
surging waves pound the ocean's shores.
Entire mountains are swept away, and the three worlds,
unanchored, start to spin and reel.
It is like the roar of towering thunderclouds
at the coming of the rains
or the resonant bursting of the cosmic egg
at the birth of time itself!

Although the king seems to have had several cannons of his own, he chose not to deploy them in penetrating the rampart walls; rather he engaged a regiment of his Muslim soldiers under the command of Kama Nayaka to lead the vanguard in dismantling the outer wall, stone by stone. As the soldiers approached, many lost their lives; cannon fire from the fort exploded all around them and shooters on the wall picked off the straggling survivors. Those that did manage to make it to the wall were at least somewhat safe, for the fort cannons were mounted in such a way that they could not be repositioned to fire on those closest to the base. With pickaxes and crowbars, the men clawed away at the wall at a dishearteningly slow pace; the loss of life was great but they beleaguered on.

And seeing how badly the attack was going, the Vijayanagara captains took to a strategy of lavishing gifts. They offered to buy stones that soldiers had pried from the walls and towers. And just to be fair, the captains paid according to the size of the stone, some were worth ten, twenty or even fifty copper coins a piece. As Nunes put it, it was by this 'device they contrived to dismantle the wall in many places, and lay the city open'. The cash incentives proved effective, for the men grew bolder with every attack. The promise of 'money had the power of freeing them from the terror of death'. After a time the captains even started offering payments for dragging away dead men from the foot of the wall. And so this steady attrition of Vijayanagara soldiers slogged on for another three months, until finally, in the summer heat of 1520, news arrived: Ismail Adil Shah and his formidable army of 1,20,000 footmen (including archers, shield bearers, spearmen and musketeers), 18,000 horses and 150 elephants had arrived from Bijapur and were setting up camp on the north bank of the Krishna. Krishnadevaraya quickly put a halt to his offensive and marched his troops to the Krishna's south bank where he set up camp and seized control of the ferries. And now, two great armies stood pitched along a mighty river, both with claim to the precious land before them. Supremacy in the western Deccan was at stake and a fearsome battle was on the horizon.

13

Battle on the Krishna

In addition to the hour-by-hour battle account provided by Nunes, the Persian historian Ferishta offers both corroborative evidence as well as new insights into the motivations of Sultan Ismail Adil Shah, the bold young ruler who took the throne of Bijapur after his father was slain in battle by Krishnadevaraya a decade earlier. Like many sultanate elites, the scholarly Ferishta was a 'Westerner', an immigrant from Central Asia, who was employed as the official court historian of the Bijapur sultanate. Unlike Nunes, however, Ferishta wrote his *Tarikh-i-Ferishta* in 1611, almost a century after the fated battle of Raichur. The text was a grand history of the Bijapur sultanate dedicated to Ismail's great grandson, Sultan Ibrahim Adil Shah II. According to Eaton, Ferishta is less trustworthy than Nunes, not only because he was further removed in time and space, but 'because he had the unenviable task of accounting for the crushing defeat of his patron's own forebear'. This kind of documentary prejudice is inevitable, especially in regard to court-patronized works, but all sources must be read within their own context and, further, against the grain of alternative records. Unfortunately, and rather surprisingly, there are no significant Telugu, Kannada or Tamil sources that document this pivotal battle, and no Hindu memory of this spectacular victory anywhere.

According to Ferishta, Ismail Adil Shah and his forces dug into their camp along the Krishna. From that secure position they anxiously awaited a Vijayanagara attack. Krishnadevaraya waited too, for there was but one ford nearby, and the mighty Krishna, even in summer, served as a natural barrier to any engagement. As night fell on 18 May 1520, a Friday evening no less, the Adil Shah was relaxing in his tent and overheard a courtier recite a couplet: 'Rise and fill the golden goblet with the wine of mirth, quick before the drinker is laid to dust!' The verse would prove strangely prophetic, for the Adil Shah, inspired by these poetic words, 'called all his favorites about him, and spreading the carpet of joy, gave way to the pleasures of music and wine'. After much revelry, the Adil Shah was so thoroughly inebriated that he decided to attack right then and there. He mounted his elephant in a drunken stupor, surveyed the river before him and ordered as many men as possible to set out on rafts. 'In vain the officers tried to convince him of the imprudence and danger of this plan; but the sultan, without a reply, plunged his own elephant into the current, and was instantly followed by his officers and soldiers on two hundred and fifty elephants.' Ismail Adil Shah's firepower was certainly superior to Vijayanagara's and he was confident that his musketeers would make short work of the unsuspecting enemy, but his rash decision to attack would prove disastrous. 'Ferishta thus framed his story as a morality play, the essential point being that the debacle had been the fault of the wine.' Nunes on the other hand offers a richer and more detailed account of the bloody encounter, with no mention of wine. The one thing both chroniclers would agree on is that the battle of Raichur was fought on the river Krishna, where the waters would soon flow crimson with the blood of Hindus, Muslims, Portuguese and countless fallen animals.

At first light on Saturday morning, news of Bijapur's advance reached the Vijayanagara camp. Krishnadevaraya immediately ordered a general advance of all his forces. Kumara Vijaya, the lord of Srirangapatnam, 'begged' that he and his thirty sons should lead the vanguard, for he was a great lord of the south, and the king's father-in-law too. And so two hours after sunrise on 19 May 1520, the first Vijayanagara line rushed to the river to meet the oncoming enemy. Since there was but one small ford nearby to cross the river, all the soldiers on both sides were forced to squeeze together into a narrow strip of the flowing river. But this is exactly what Ismail Adil Shah had intended, for he was ready to repel any counterattack with his superior firepower. And with no hesitation on account of the inevitable collateral loss of life, the Adil Shah ordered a relentless barrage of gunfire and cannon. Kumara Vijaya and his men, along with many soldiers of Bijapur, were mowed down en masse. Seeing the great carnage, many abandoned their charge and retreated, others fanned out along the river, and a general confusion set in among the Vijayanagara troops. The Adil Shah now took the opportunity to charge. The onslaught was fierce; there was nothing but blood and slaughter for half a league, and Krishnadevaraya's shattered troops began to flee.

When the king saw his men in flight, he yelled, 'Traitors! Now I see who sides with me!' He rode out before his ranks and cried, 'We all die one day, one way or another. Let us meet fate boldly and find death in battle like our heroic fathers! The day has arrived. The Adil Shah may boast he has slain the greatest lord in the world, but never that he had vanquished him!' He took out a ring from his finger and gave it to one of his pages, so that it might be shown to the king's queens as a token of his death, and so they might burn themselves according to custom. Then the king reared his mighty steed and cried out, 'Now! Who ranges himself with me?!' With this rallying call, Krishnadevaraya charged into the breach. And all his captains, newly inspired by their fearless lord, joined his side to do battle.

By this point, the Bijapuri troops had also broken rank; men and animals in and along the river were in complete disarray. As Nunes puts it, 'The confusion was so great amongst the Moors and such havoc was wrought in their ranks that they did not even try to defend the camp they had made so strong and enclosed so well. Like lost men they leaped into the river to save themselves. After them came large numbers of the king's troops and elephants. The latter worked mischief without end, for they seized men with their trunks and tore them into small pieces, while their riders in their little castle-like howdahs killed countless more.' What seemed like an easy victory for Ismail Adil Shah had quickly turned into a devastating rout. Although Ferishta declares that 'the heroes of Islam, as if animated with one soul, behaved so gallantly' and felled over a thousand infidels, the Vijayanagara troops were too many and the Bijapuris were eventually put to flight. As Eaton poetically puts it, 'Ismail found himself trapped between two Krishnas: before him the king of

Vijayanagara, and to his rear the swirling currents of the Krishna river.'

There was hysteria everywhere: many drowned in the river, massive elephants with deadly spears strapped to their tusks roamed directionless without their masters, mutilated bodies littered the bloody riverbanks, and whosoever was left alive scrambled to escape the mayhem. Seeing the gruesome and bloody scene, Krishnadevaraya, 'out of compassion', commanded his troops to stand down. Immediately, all the captains obeyed and each withdrew his forces. While the Bijapuris fled for safer ground, Krishnadevaraya crossed the river and marched triumphantly into Ismail Adil Shah's camp. He rested in the sultan's tent with his war council, and when his ministers urged him to pursue the sultan and his troops, the king responded, 'Too many who were not to blame have died here today. If the Adil Shah has done me wrong, he has suffered enough. Besides, the unclaimed fort of Raichur remains behind us. We should take it before any advance, so make ready to capture the fort. This time we will have a new and better strategy!'

First the troops scoured the battlefield to collect the spoils of battle. From the Bijapuri camp they claimed 4,000 horses from Hormuz, 100 elephants, 400 heavy and light cannons, 900 gun carriages and many richly decorated tents. As Nunes adds, 'I take no account of the sumpter-horses and oxen and other beasts, for they were numberless, nor of the numbers of men and boys, nor yet of some women, whom the king ordered to be released.' As for the Adil Shah, he was nowhere to be found; he had never even entered the fray. During the battle, the lord of Belgaum named Asada Khan, who had sensed the imminent defeat, rallied around the sultan with his 400 cavalrymen and screamed, 'Sire, if you wish to live, follow me!' And with these words Asada Khan lifted his lord on to an elephant and helped him escape.

Another outcome of the battle was the capture of Salabat Khan, captain general of the Adil Shah's troops. Unlike his master, Salabat Khan had rallied his disheartened men and fought to the bitter end. As Nunes proudly records, the sultan and his select guard of 500 Portuguese renegades did 'such wonderful deeds' with 'their terrible strokes', but alas they all perished, and Salabat Khan, like 'a furious wolf amongst sheep', was finally taken hostage. Noteworthy is the mention of Portuguese renegades, men who had left the service of King Dom Manuel of Portugal and found employ at various Indian courts. These men were guns for hire, with no allegiances to anyone but themselves. As we will soon see, another band of Portuguese mercenaries would prove indispensable to Krishnadevaraya and his siege efforts.

The king stayed at the Bijapuri camp till all the dead

had been burned and the funerary honours had been paid. In memory of the 16,000 souls who had perished in the battle, he gave much in alms to the local residents. And with these things done, he turned once again upon Raichur and pitched his camp as he had done before. On his return, Krishnadevaraya had a fortuitous encounter with one Christovão de Figueiredo, a Portuguese nobleman on his way to Vijayanagara to trade in horses. He was accompanied by a brigade of twenty Portuguese musketeers whom the king took much pleasure in meeting. He was glad that Figueiredo and his men would 'witness the war and his great power'. He ordered that they be given the fine new tents taken from the Adil Shah's camp, and had them lodged close to his own quarters. Krishnadevaraya seems to have greatly enjoyed Figueiredo's company, and one day as they talked in the royal tent, Figueiredo asked if he could go and see the Moors under siege at the fort. Krishnadevaraya refused as he was concerned for his new friend's safety, but Figueiredo quickly replied, 'The whole business of the Portuguese is war! Letting me go would be the greatest favour that you could do upon me.' And upon hearing these words, the king relented and sent a few men to accompany Figueiredo and his men to the trenches near the wall.

As Nunes describes, Figueiredo saw how fearlessly the Moors exposed themselves on the high fort walls.

They moved about carefree because they'd never faced a weapon that could reach far enough to harm them. With gusto, Figueiredo and his snipers found a place to hide and opened fire with their long-distance, high-precision Portuguese muskets. They picked off many Moors, and the king's men found a welcome opportunity to approach the wall in safety. And soon enough the soldiers resumed their earlier work of chipping away at the masonry and dismantling the fort wall. The muskets the Portuguese carried were of rare quality, able to shoot from a greater distance and with far more accuracy than anyone in these parts had ever witnessed. They were most probably from the 'Indo-Portuguese' tradition of matchlocks, a rather new but innovative amalgamation of Muslim cannon technology, Portuguese artillery knowledge and the masterful gun-making engineers of Goa. In was no coincidence then that the battle of Raichur was the first major conflict in the Indian interior in which European mercenaries participated, and the first documented usage of firearms in the Deccan.

When Krishnadevaraya heard that the Portuguese had 'entered the city', he rushed to the wall to see the scene for himself. This was the opportunity that Krishnadevaraya had been waiting for; and so with the Portuguese musketeers covering him from behind, the king and his men could approach the citadel unharassed. It was likely this moment that inspired the king to write: 'When a king presses an enemy army into a corner, there is no turning from heaven or victory! There are mechanized weapons of various design to penetrate rampart walls and send in troops.'

Now Figueiredo divided his musketeers into three companies and killed any Moor who dared show himself on the wall. Soon the king's troops, who had divided themselves into three similar divisions, were breaking down the wall with pickaxes and crowbars. Fort defenders began to abandon the first line of the fortification; women and children hid themselves. As Nunes records, the captain of the city, seeing the dismay that was spreading all around, tried to calm his people down with encouraging words. Finally, he repaired to the part of the wall that seemed most severely pressed and exclaimed, 'The first Portuguese to show himself, is a dead man!' Wishing to see for himself where the Portuguese were stationed, he stuck his head out above the parapet, and just like that, he was shot dead, by a musket ball straight to the middle of his forehead. Curiosity killed the captain, and Figueiredo himself is said to have fired the fatal blow. And with the captain's demise, the city wept, for Raichur was left defenceless.

The next day, about three weeks after the river battle with the Adil Shah, the men of Raichur opened the city gate, and with a white flag outstretched before them, walked to the king's camp with their hands uplifted, begging for mercy. When they arrived before him, they 'prostrated themselves on the ground with much groaning and tears, and besought his pity and benevolence'. Krishnadevaraya bid them rise, saying that he would spare all their lives and possessions. 'You have nothing to fear,' he said. 'Return to the city and I shall enter it tomorrow.' And while the people of Raichur were still in the king's presence, they saw 'Christovao de Figueiredo, and told the king that the conquest and capture of the city was due to that foreigner'. The king cast his eyes on Figueiredo, nodded his head, and turned to the people saying, 'See what great things can be effected by one good man!' And it was true – a siege that could have lasted years was over in a matter of weeks. When all was said and done, the king retired to his tent, and the men of the city to the city, while the Vijayanagara troops made merry with much feasting and rejoicing.

And so the following morning, after all the requisite pujas were complete, Krishnadevaraya entered the city of Raichur in triumph. The city folk raised their hands to heaven and cried, 'God be praised for sending us such a savior after so many years!' It was not long before news of Krishnadevaraya's astounding victory reached the courts of the other four sultanates of Berar, Bidar, Ahmadnagar and Golconda. All the sultans sent envoys to praise the king's success, saying how astonished they were to hear that such a great city had fallen, and even more surprised to learn of the king's mighty army. Whatever goodwill the Deccan sultans had had before the battle of Raichur now quickly turned to fear. They had earlier supported Krishnadevaraya's attack on Bijapur, but they had not expected such a devastating victory. As the Portuguese proverb warns, 'When you see your neighbor's beard on fire, better soak your own in water!' And so it was that Krishnadevaraya's retaking of Raichur made him the greatest lord of the Deccan, for from east to west, everything south of the Krishna river was the undisputed sovereign realm of Vijayanagara.

The king stayed in the city for a few days making arrangements for the city's governance. For the people's protection, he commanded the wall to be repaired, and fresh troops to be stationed in the citadel. And to those citizens who wished to leave, he showed great mercy and even offered them provisions for their journey. Then, with his new Portuguese friends as honoured guests, Krishnadevaraya returned to the capital, where his stunning triumph was celebrated with grand feasts and much entertainment.

14

City and Palace

As they returned to Vijayanagara, Krishnadevaraya and his queens, along with his high lords, veered a league south of the royal centre to their new mansions in Nagalapura, the recently constructed royal suburb that the king named in honour of his cherished mother. Krishnadevaraya held the Portuguese in high regard for having aided his men in Raichur, and arranged for his honoured guests to be lodged in some very fine mansions. Indeed, the king's earlier contact with the Portuguese Friar Luis had been lukewarm, but now, after a decade of witnessing the steady rise of the Portuguese in Goa, Krishnadevaraya resolved to secure an alliance with this new power from the West. By now Afonso de Albuquerque had wrested control of all the major seaways that brought valued warhorses into the Deccan. The king was thus eager to strike an agreement with his new horse-trading friends. Moreover, he sought to secure an exclusive trade deal by outbidding his enemies, particularly the sultan of Bijapur. A verse from the king's poems on governance sums up his position best: 'Merchants from distant lands, who import elephants and warhorses should be kept in imperial service at the capital. Treat them with prestige and provide them with towns and mansions. Purchase their goods at a high price and ensure that your enemies are deprived of such resources.'

Luckily for us, an inquisitive horse-trader named Domingo Paes was part of Christovão de Figueiredo's party. His memoirs offer us a rare and detailed picture of court life during Vijayanagara's heyday. In addition, his special audience with the king provides an unprecedented eyewitness portrait of Krishnadevaraya. As the verse above intimates, Paes and the other Portuguese were treated with princely hospitality. The king dispatched his most trusted lords and captains to visit the Portuguese and make them feel welcome. He sent to their mansions many sheep and fowls, and several pots full of butter, honey and other things to eat. One day, Figueiredo and the others were invited to a private audience with the king. And so the Portuguese made their way to the royal chambers, all handsomely dressed in their best finery, holding many delightful gifts from their homeland for the king. For his part, the king received them with his characteristic grace, enthusiasm and curiosity. As Paes describes, Krishnadevaraya said many kind and pleasant things to Figueiredo. He asked after his well-being, and was curious to learn of 'the kind of state which the king of Portugal kept up'. On hearing of Dom Manuel and his empire, the king seemed much pleased with Figueiredo; he doted on him and looked upon him 'as if he had been one of his own people'. Paes records that the king showed great kindness to the whole party. He describes how they were all seated so close to the king that he 'touched us all, and could not have enough of looking at us'. Certainly there was a mutual sense of wonder and respect that animated the proceedings.

Paes goes on to provide a detailed description of the king's royal attire. He was decked in fine white clothes ornamented with golden roses, and wore around his neck a diamond necklace of very great value. This matches quite well with Krishnadevaraya's own verse about kingly attire: 'A king should don a single gem whose luster shines throughout the world. He should wear the finest clothes embroidered with sparkling silver, and ornament himself with matching jewels according to the day of the week.' Upon his head was a brocade cap of the finest silk which reminded Paes of a war helmet from his native Iberia. And last but not least, he was barefoot, 'for no one ever enters where the king is unless one has bare feet'. This intimate encounter with the great king of Vijayanagara left a deep impression on Paes. He memorialized Krishnadevaraya as 'the most feared and perfect king that could possibly be, cheerful of disposition and very merry. He seeks to honour foreigners, and receives them kindly . . . so gallant and perfect is he in all things!' And when it was time for the guests to return to their quarters, Krishnadevaraya offered Figueiredo a brocade tunic along with a cap in the same fashion as his own. And to each of the other guests he gifted 'a cloth embroidered with many pretty figures'. And by this gesture, it was clear to Paes that the king acted not out of formality, but as a 'token of friendship and love'.

One day during their stay, Figueiredo begged a kindness of the king. He wished to be shown the palace, saying his officers would rejoice at having something to tell their friends should they return home by the grace of god. And at once Krishnadevaraya commanded that the Portuguese be given a tour of the palace, except for the women's quarters, which 'no one ever sees'. Their guide was the trusted Gandaraja, brother of Timmarasu, who escorted the men through a side gate of the palace, a service entrance so to speak, 'by which the ladies serving the king's wives enter and exit during the feasts'. His wide-eyed account of Vijayanagara is a priceless portal into an unimaginable empire, never to be forgotten if ever it was to be believed. As Paes himself admits, 'I cannot possibly describe it all, nor should I be believed if I tried to do so. I have no words to express what I saw. To try and tell of what I saw is hopeless, for I went around with my head so often turned from one side to the other that I almost fell over with my senses lost!' What follows is a paraphrased excerpt of Paes's vivid recollection of the Vijayanagara royal enclosure:

> They made us stand still, and they counted us one by one as they ushered us into a small courtyard with a smoothly plastered floor and bright white walls. At the end of the courtyard are two gates, one open and the other closed. The latter is the king's residence where the sides of the entrance are painted with two life-size images, one a likeness of the king, and the other of his father. The father was dark, a gentleman of fine form, but stouter than the son. Both figures stand decked in full regalia. And when we wished to continue through the open gate, they counted us yet again, and only then did we enter a wing of the palace living quarters.
>
> It is like a little mansion with many chambers. One room has two little steps covered with gilded copper that lead to a porch enclosed by a railing of heart-shaped stones fashioned with rubies, diamonds and pearls. Another chamber has a canopy bed gilded with gold and fitted with a railing of pearls. There's a mattress covered in black satin,

two cushions and nothing else. We saw another chamber with cross-beams and stone pillars topped with ivory carvings of roses and lotuses. All the craftsmanship was so well executed, one could not find better anywhere in the world. Most interesting are the mansion walls which are painted with images from life at court. We could even see ourselves depicted in one of the murals! The king's artists paint these so the women of the palace may see the goings on of the outside world.

In another building, underneath some arches, there is a little door chained closed with many padlocks. They told us that inside was a treasury of one of the former kings. When we left this structure we entered a courtyard (like an arena for beast-fights!) with pillars made of wood and large cross beams gilded with copper. From this area we climbed four or five steps and toured some very beautiful houses made in the way I have already told you.

Later we saw a fine structure built with many stone pillars, and you must know that they make no use of this building because it belongs to their idol and to the temple. The idol is kept safe behind a closed door, and whenever they celebrate any festival, they carry this idol under a canopy on a golden throne accompanied by brahmans who perform the ceremonies, and dancing girls who come to dance. Moving along, we passed through a corridor and mounted stairs where we saw three caldrons of gold, each

> large enough to cook half a cow! And finally, we went up a little staircase and through a little door into a magnificent hall, where the king sends women to be trained in dance.
>
> It is a long hall, not very wide, with stone sculptures on pillars supported by plinths carved with great beasts like elephants. Along the walls are decorative panels painted with colorful images of stags and elephants, and dancing girls with little drums. The panels also show all the proper dance positions, particularly the pose that ends the dance, and this is to teach the women, and help them in case they forget anything. And at the end of the hall is a painted recess where the women stretch and loosen their bodies and legs. They train to make their whole body supple in order for their dancing to be more graceful. And at the other end, on the right, is a lounge with walls and floors of gold where the king sits to watch.
>
> They did not show us more than this. The residence of the women no man may see except the eunuchs. So from here we returned by the way we entered, and there again they counted us once more.

Paes, Figueiredo and the other Portuguese were so enamoured with Vijayanagara and the fine pleasures of city life that they stayed on for some months, enough to witness the great Mahanavami or Navaratri festival celebrated every autumn. It was the most important event of the year, for these weeks of celebration brought together all aspects of imperial life, from elaborate pujas and public entertainment to a review of troops and the payment of salaries. And of course, luxurious feasting, for if there was one phrase that Paes repeats more than any other in his description of the festival it is 'and now, returning to the feasts!' Indeed, the Navaratri festival was a perfect blend of the social, cultural, religious and political life of the kingdom, all wrapped into one non-stop celebration lasting for much longer than its namesake nine nights.

All the king's chief lords along with all their respective retainers arriving in the capital were housed in giant tents erected near the palace walls. And every morning for nine days the king would arrive near the Bhuvana Vijayam to perform the morning pujas. Before him came some twenty horses, fully decked out and saddled with cloths embroidered with gold and precious stones, for 'they show off well the grandeur and state of their king'. All the lords filed in to 'make their salaam' to Krishnadevaraya who was seated on a throne fashioned of gold and precious stones. At the centre of this display of imperial fealty was Timmarasu, whom the king looked upon as a father. He stationed himself at the gate and supervised the whole affair. Next came the priests carrying boiled rice, cooked edibles, water, fire and many kinds of fragrances which they used to conduct their elaborate rituals. Both Nunes and Paes describe how the rites were often accompanied by great sacrificial slaughter. Paes informs us that Krishnadevaraya witnessed the slaughter of twenty-four buffaloes and 150 sheep, all of which were offered as a sacrifice to the idol. He adds, 'You must know that they cut off the heads of these buffaloes and sheep at one blow with certain large sickles which are wielded by a man who has charge of this slaughter; he is so sure of hand that not a single blow misses.'

On certain days, the idols would be finely decorated, placed in a giant chariot, and pulled through city lanes in a glorious procession. The festive atmosphere seems to have reminded Paes of the Corpo de Dios festival celebrated in his native Lisbon. Behind the idol would follow hundreds of skilled dancing girls, for they played an especially important role in all state and religious functions. All of them were fair and young, from sixteen to twenty years of age, some of them so heavily bedecked with bracelets and jewels that their arms needed to be supported by other women. And last would come the massive elephants in full decoration as the idol wended its way back to the Bhuvana Vijayam where the king performed yet more pujas, followed by more sacrifices and even more dancing. And then there was dinner, a most grand and sumptuous banquet, for the king fasted during those nine days and only ate at midnight. And with the feasting came the spectacular evening entertainment when the whole palace was filled with flickering torches. There were plays, water sports, mock battles, colourful 'rockets' and fireworks, and gory wrestling matches to boot in which huge men struck at each other with knuckledusters, delivering blows severe enough to break teeth, put out eyes and disfigure faces. Incapacitated contenders would be carried off silently by their friends while judges honoured winners with a silken cloth of victory.

A few days after the festival came the annual review of the armed forces and the paying of officer salaries. It was an impressive event, for the troops that guarded the city alone stood at some 50,000 men including shield bearers, spearmen and archers, not to mention thousands of the finest stallions and hundreds of elephants in all their colourful trappings. In a glorious procession the king would set out for a specially erected tent a full league from the city. From this vantage point he would watch as his captains marched out towards him according to rank with their troops arrayed in perfect formation. It was a grand public display of martial prowess designed to further glorify the empire and its sovereign lord. As Paes witnessed, 'The king passed along gazing at his soldiers, who gave great shouts and cries and struck their shields. The horses neighed, the elephants screamed, and it seemed as if the city would be turned upside down! The hills and valleys and all the ground trembled with the firing of guns and muskets; and to see the bombs and fire-missiles over the plains, this was indeed wonderful. Truly it seemed as if the whole world were collected there! I was so carried away with myself, it felt like I was in a dream.'

Part of the men's excitement must have come from the fact that the spectacle was also occasion for the payment of annual salaries. Captains would renew their pledges of fealty and the king would distribute, all according to rank, thousands upon thousands of pardaos. These gold coins struck in the Vijayanagara mint had an image of the king on one side and the imperial boar insignia on the other. For this reason they are also known as *varahas*, from the Sanskrit word for boar. The currency was valued and accepted all throughout the Deccan, and particularly in Portuguese Goa. But for the soldiers of Vijayanagara, the annual gift from the king was their rightful due, a token of recognition for their loyal service to king and country. That day they rallied around their lord and rejoiced with him, believing full well that they served the most glorious emperor that ever was.

15

The Final Years

The mood at the Vijayanagara capital was indeed jubilant, for by 1520 Krishnadevaraya had established himself as the undisputed ruler of the south. And now, a decade into his reign, the king could finally spend more time at home among his people in his magnificent city. One thing we know Krishnadevaraya engaged himself with during these years was public works projects, perhaps as a way to give back to the people who had supported him all along. In addition to the building of new temples and the restoration of others, the king busied himself with the construction of several waterworks, in particular the great tank for his new suburb of Nagalapura (modern-day Hospet). As he declared in a verse:

The root purpose of an expansive empire
is the acquisition of wealth.
But no matter how big your empire is
build tanks and canals for the benefit of farmers,
Ease taxes and grain revenues, be strong,
and both *artha* and *dharma* will grow.

The massive tank and its intricate piping system was constructed with the help of a Portuguese engineer named João della Ponte who was 'a great worker in stone'. Upon completion, this important new source of fresh water 'made many improvements in the city'; several channels were dug to water rice fields and flower gardens, and on top of that, the newly irrigated lands were given tax-free to the people for nine years.

But amid these public projects, there arrived an ambassador named Matucotam, dispatched by the disgruntled Adil Shah of Bijapur to negotiate a settlement between the two empires. But Krishnadevaraya, feigning ignorance of his arrival, kept him waiting for a whole month before granting the weary envoy a private audience. Finally, when the ambassador was called to court, he arrived with a handsome party of his countrymen to convey their lord's message. He said, 'Sire! My master the Adil Shah bids me say that he bears no ill will towards you. He believes you to be the most powerful prince in all the world, and one possessed of much justice. But since you broke peace without reason, he requests that you return his artillery and tents, his horses and elephants, and restore his city of Raichur.' The king pondered for a time and calmly replied, 'I would be happy to restore everything to the Adil Shah, including his general Salabat Khan whom I hold captive, under one condition: Ismail Adil Shah must come here and kiss my foot.'

Upon hearing such an insolent request, Matucotam, without a word, took his leave and conveyed the audacious message to his master. The Adil Shah responded that he was willing to do so, but since it was impossible for him to enter enemy territory he would be unable to fulfil the king's wish. And to this Krishnadevaraya retorted, 'So be it, if the Adil Shah is unwilling to come to me, I shall go to him!' And with these words the king set out north with all his men, anxious to meet the Adil Shah face to face. After over a decade of crushing victories, Krishnadevaraya was undefeated in battle. He had raised Vijayanagara to the apex of its power and he was determined now to prove his supremacy over the Deccan sultans once and for all. Krishnadevaraya's meteoric rise from ambitious upstart to haughty conqueror suggests signs of a growing megalomania. And coupled with his 'sudden fits of rage' which Paes seems to have witnessed at first hand, the immense power that Krishnadevaraya now commanded was going to his head. The 'kiss-my-foot demand' crossed a line and now the king was marching to cross another, for when the Adil Shah failed to meet him, Krishnadevaraya crossed the Krishna into Bijapur territory, leaving behind a wake of pillage and destruction.

Like a wave of plunder, Krishnadevaraya and his forces swept through Kembavi, Nirmanuru, Sagara, Bijapur and finally Gulbarga, the erstwhile Bahmani capital. Nunes mentions some of these events, but the most interesting information comes from three verses in Krishnadevaraya's *Amuktamalyada*. His bold first-person voice carries a powerful sense of purpose and conviction. For example, he poetically (if not gruesomely) describes the attack on the town of Kembavi, which in Telugu means red water tank. 'I, Krishna Raya, lord of the earth, gave true meaning to the name of Kembavi in the language of Andhra, for the water tanks here are crimson red, filled with blood of Yavanas! Standing at the front of my army, I toppled the high fort walls that once blocked the path of rain clouds!' A similar tone follows as he describes the city of Nirmanuru by proclaiming, 'I, Krishna Raya, lord of the earth stood at the front of my army, and led a stampede of ferocious elephants against the Yavana king, toppling his shining jeweled mansions that rise to kiss the sky.' As Krishnadevaraya unrelentingly pursued his enemy, a panicked Adil Shah vacated his fine capital of Bijapur, 'the best city in all the kingdom of Deccan'. Among its many beautiful houses were vineyards and green gardens with trees full of pomegranates, oranges and lemons. But soon the fair city would be 'left almost in ruins'. Krishnadevaraya took up residence in the palace, and while he ordered no attack, he seems to have done nothing when his men, under the pretence of looking for firewood, looted and ransacked the city through and through. Somehow the gentle mercy that the king had once shown to the citizenry now gave way to an apathetic disregard for civil violence.

And if this was not enough, Krishnadevaraya continued his rabid pursuit, straight to Gulbarga, the traditional seat of the Bahmanis, where his men pillaged the city and razed the fortress to the ground. This was no longer a move against the Adil Shah alone; by going all the way to the original Bahmani capital of Gulbarga, Krishnadevaraya was posturing to all the sultans of the Deccan. And although religion appears nowhere as a motivation for Krishnadevaraya's actions, there was a very clear sense that these enemies, unlike his nemesis the Gajapati, were of a different faith. Inside the fortress of Gulbarga, the king found three sons of the long-dead Bahmani sultan Mahmud Shah. These disenfranchised brothers had apparently been imprisoned by the five Deccan sultans when they had subverted Bahmani authority around a decade earlier. Krishnadevaraya took it upon himself to raise the eldest son to the position of sultan. Now the king of Vijayanagara believed himself powerful enough to dictate the succession line of his enemies. This bold act, which was more about power than religion, garnered him the Telugu epithet *yavana-sthapincavadu*, or the Establisher of Yavana Rule. This final gesture proved that Krishnadevaraya was supreme ruler of the Deccan, but his excessive pride was growing out of control, and it was making him enemies.

Krishnadevaraya was eager to push further north into sultanate lands, but luckily his wise councillors convinced him otherwise. They urged the king not to upset the other sultans, for those 'lords would probably make friends with the Adil Shah and rise up together against the king'. Thankfully the king relented, for the advice of his war council was not only sage, but prophetic. In less than fifty years, the Deccan sultans would indeed unite as a single force against Vijayanagara. The seeds of animosity the king had sown in the ashes of this rampage would soon ripen, but not in his lifetime. It would be in 1565, during the turbulent reign of Krishnadevaraya's son-in-law Ramaraya, when the sultans would finally exact their revenge. In the infamous battle of Talikota, just twenty-five leagues south of Bijapur, the armies of Vijayanagara would be crushed by an alliance of all five

Deccan sultans. Ramaraya would be beheaded on the battlefield and the sultans would march on the capital of Vijayanagara. And finding the city abandoned, the troops would quickly transform the glorious metropolis into a smouldering ruin of wood and stone. And just like that Vijayanagara would be no more.

Krishnadevaraya could not foresee this tragic fate, for pride had blinded him. He was wrapped up in his stunning victories and steady accumulation of power. As Eaton observes, the kiss-my-foot incident 'serves to humanize the man, and as such can perhaps provide a much-needed corrective to the king's idealized, cardboard cut-out image found in most textbooks'. He further argues: 'Nunes's account of Krishna Raya's overbearing behavior in the aftermath of the Raichur battle stands at odds with his image in modern scholarship, which tends to revere him as an ideal Indian monarch – heroic, virtuous, pious, and just.' Indeed, Krishnadevaraya's image in popular imagination is one of a romantic, godlike monarch. Even in his own time the king was praised as 'god Krishna born again into the world!' And as the legends grew, even his name changed: from Krishnaraya as it is recorded in the medieval sources to Krishnadevaraya, and later always Sri Krishnadevaraya. No doubt the current biography also paints a rather glowing picture of the king, for he was indeed an iconic, larger-than-life man of history, and therefore also an imperfect human being. For Krishnadevaraya, his pride would lead to ruin, not for him or his personal legacy, but his hard-won empire.

After Gulbarga, Nunes tell us that 'nothing worthy of record' passed between Krishnadevaraya and the Adil Shah relating to either peace or war. Finally there was a time of calm and Krishnadevaraya proudly returned to his capital to enjoy the great empire which he had fought so tirelessly to gain. Regarding these last years of Krishnadevaraya's life, the historical archive grows quiet while the whispers of legend grow loud. It was now 1523, the king was in his mid- to late forties, and 'feeling advanced in years' and 'desiring to rest in his old age', he wished to appoint a successor while still sound of body. His son Tirumalaraya, son of his chief queen Tirumaladevi, was now about six years old, and in order to ensure his succession, Krishnadevaraya abdicated the Lion Throne of Vijayanagara and installed his son as the new king. He would now serve as chief minister to the boy-king and Timmarasu was demoted to the rank of councillor. This seemingly premature gesture was probably precipitated by growing intrigues at court, particularly the schemings of the king's ambitious son-in-law Ramaraya who was secretly plotting to seize the throne for himself. After crowning the young boy with his own hands,

Krishnadevaraya called for great festivals which lasted for eight months, during which time the boy suddenly fell sick and died. Poisoning was suspected and the blame fell on the most unlikely of people: the king's most beloved minister Timmarasu.

Oral tradition maintains that the ageing but still influential minister was cunningly framed, either by Ramaraya or perhaps the Gajapati, but whatever the case may be, Krishnadevaraya seems to have accepted the false accusation of murder at face value. He called for Timmarasu and addressed him, 'I have always held you as my great friend. For forty years you have governed this kingdom which you gave to me. I realize now that when you gave me the crown, you were disloyal to my brother, and therefore a traitor. And now you and your sons have poisoned my son!' And with these words he had Timmarasu, along with his sons and brother, seized and imprisoned. Nunes records that they languished in prison for three years, perhaps in the stronghold of Penukonda which even today boasts a signboard for 'Timmarasu's Jail'. This rather sad tale gets even worse, 'for in this country they do not put brahmans to death but only inflict some punishment so that they remain alive'. And so finally, for the capital crime of regicide, the king ordered that Timmarasu be blinded with a burning rod of iron. In a tragic and ironic twist of fate, Krishnadevaraya put out the eyes of the man who had earlier saved his own. The 1962 Telugu film *Mahamantri Timmarasu* dramatizes the fateful moment in the final scene. As Krishnadevaraya comes to his senses and learns the truth of Timmarasu's innocence, he cries out in agony, 'Appaji! Appaji!', begging forgiveness from the man who was a father to him. It was a grievous episode in the twilight of Krishnadevaraya's reign, and it presaged even more disastrous events to come.

There is surprisingly little historical information available about the king's final years. There were no battles or uprisings of note, but Krishnadevaraya remained ever vigilant even from the comfort of his capital, watching over his enemies like a sloth bear in the high treetops, sleeping with one eye open. News from the north would have reached him – an enterprising warlord from Samarkand named Babur had vanquished the Lodi dynasty at Panipat in 1526. With the coming of the Mughals, the whole political configuration of the north was on the brink of change, but Krishnadevaraya would witness none of it. Nunes tells us that while the king was busy making plans with the Portuguese to attack the Bijapuri city of Belgaum in 1529, 'he fell sick with the same illness as his ancestors, with pains in the groin, of which die all the kings of Vijayanagara'. This may seem a bathetic end, but the king died as he lived, in the unrelenting pursuit of empire. Oral tradition tells us that upon Krishnadevaraya's demise, his court poet and trusted friend Peddana lamented that he could not accompany his beloved patron to heaven. He would have to carry on, like a living corpse.

Another verse from Peddana effusively captures the idealized memory of Krishnadevaraya's enlightened reign. It reads:

O Krishnaraya, Lord of the Earth,
    son of Narasimha and grandson of Ishvara!
You are endowed with great beauty, and when you ruled
    the whole empire prospered and flourished!
You allayed your people's anxieties about ominous comets,
    and freed them of their fear of torrential rains.
During your reign even barren lands witnessed rain
    three times a month!
You overran the capital cities of haughty kings
    and saved your people
    from the terror of marauding invaders.
The very thought of sin disappeared
    from the minds of your subjects!
All good people, from children to cowherds,
    lived happily and thrived.
And every citizen prospered
    as if Lord Rama himself was ruling!

Like all celebrated kings, Krishnadevaraya was a man of the people. In a verse from his writing on political theory, he enjoins that a king should care for the empire like his own body, for the two are one. In another stanza the king writes: 'A king must listen to the cries of the destitute and care for their needs. He must always be ready to protect his people, for if a king keeps the welfare of the people in his heart, the people will care for the welfare of the king.' Krishnadevaraya saw the empire and his people as a reflection of his own being, as a symbiotic relationship between king and subject. As an ancient Tamil poem reads, 'Not rice, not water, only the king is the life-breath of a kingdom. And it is the duty of a king with his army of spears to know he's the life of the wide, blossoming kingdom.' Indeed, more than all of his stunning military exploits, it was Krishnadevaraya's noble and generous character that caused people to love him, both then and now. History is good at remembering a king's victories and defeats, but it is people who forever carry on the memory of a king's character. This popular legacy may or may not be historically accurate, but it is surely meaningful, for it captures how people want their leaders to be: bold, just and inspiring.

One of the last recorded acts of the king was the dedication of a breathtaking Narasimha statue that continues to inspire onlookers to this day. The impressive monolith was officially consecrated on the auspicious lunar eclipse day of 2 April 1528 in accordance with all the prescribed rituals by one Arya Krishna Bhatta, the king's domestic priest. According to the Kannada inscription nearby, Krishnaraya Maharaya 'having given away gold and poured out water', thrice repeated the phrase *na mama*, 'Not mine, not mine, not mine!' And although this was a customary declaration of giving, there is a sense that Krishnadevaraya could feel his end drawing near. He was acknowledging that the empire was not his, but the people's. One Kannada source states: 'A king should rule his kingdom in such a way as to make his name remembered even after his death.' And in that spirit, Krishnadevaraya decreed that the villages of Vanganuru and Belachinte be made rent-free and tax-free for as long as the sun and moon shall endure.

For centuries the image was known as Ugra Narasimha, the ferocious aspect of Vishnu's man-lion avatar. Later, however, it was discovered that the image was in fact Lakshmi Narasimha, a gentler and kinder manifestation of the deity. Even today one can see the broken arm of Vishnu that once embraced Lakshmi seated on his lap. The message is that the terrifying and the loving could exist together, even reinforce each other in a single being. In those final years, Krishnadevaraya surely looked back on his incredible life, one filled with both bloodshed and peace, cruelty and compassion, love and war. Some of the last poems penned by the king read:

> There's no atoning for one's sins
> after ruling over an empire!
> Seek eternal refuge in god,
> for that is the only way to counter the proverb
> *rajyante narakam dhruvam*
> 'Hell surely awaits at the end of empire!'
> The Vedas don't tell us to do the impossible,
> they only say do the best you can.

And his best was truly remarkable, unimaginable even. Today, among the silent ruins of Hampi, the past still whispers stories of a king, his people and his empire. You can hear them at twilight, on the ghats of the Virupaksha temple along the babbling Tungabhadra river, when the setting sun turns the rocky hills a magical golden red. The legendary life of Krishnadevaraya of Vijayanagara is a timely reminder of what true leadership can be, and how one charismatic figure can shape the course of history. Some day the crumbling ruins of Vijayanagara are sure to disappear, but the memory of the empire's most celebrated king will scarcely be forgotten.

Bibliography

Primary texts and translations

Birch, Walter de Gray (trans.). *The Commentaries of the Great Afonso Dalboquerque (Volume I)*. London: Hakluyt Society (1875).

Birch, Walter de Gray (trans.). *The Commentaries of the Great Afonso Dalboquerque (Volume II)*. London: Hakluyt Society (1877).

Briggs, John. *History of the Rise of the Mahomedan Power in India*. Delhi: Low Price Publications (1829, reprint).

Chandrasekhara Reddi, D. *Śrī Kṛṣṇadevarāya Vaibhavam*. Hyderabad: Telugu Samiti (2010).

Dames, Mansel Longworth. *The Book of Duarte Barbosa*. London: Hakluyt Society (1918–21).

Hultzsch, E. *Indian Antiquary*, *Epigraphia Indica*, South Indian Inscriptions (1892).

Mukku Timmana. *Pārijātāpaharaṇamu*. Chennapuri: Vavilla Ramaswamishastrulu and Sons (1968).

Nandi Timmana. *Pārijātāpaharaṇamu with Parimalollasamu*. Kuppam: Dravida University (2006).

Ramachandra Rao, C.V. *Rāyavācakamu*. Hyderabad: Andhra Pradesh Sahitya Akademi (1982).

Rao, T. Koteswara. *Āmuktamālyada Saundaryalahari Vyākhyānam*. Hyderabad: T. Koteswara Rao (2001).

Reddy, Srinivas (trans.). *Giver of the Worn Garland: Sri Krishnadevaraya's Amuktamalyada*. New Delhi: Penguin Books (2010).

Reddy, Srinivas (trans.). 'Tale of the Untouchable Devotee from Kṛṣṇadevarāya's *Āmuktamālyada*'. *Sagar: A South Asian Research Journal*, Spring 2014, Vol. 22, pp. 2–41.

Sewell, Robert. *A Forgotten Empire (Vijayanagar): A Contribution to the History of India*. London: Swan Sonnenschien & Co. (1900).

Sistla, Srinivas (trans.). *Allasani Peddana Manu Charitra*. Visakhapatnam: Drusya Kala Deepika (2012).

Sistla, Srinivas (trans.). *Sri Krishna Deva Raya Amuktamalyada*. Visakhapatnam: Drusya Kala Deepika (2010).

Venkataraya Sastri, Vedamu. *Āmuktamālyada Āndhra-vyākhyāna sahitamu*. Madras: Vedamu Venkatarayasastri and Brothers (1964).

Wagoner, Phillip B. (trans.). *Tidings of the King: A Translation and Ethnohistorical Analysis of the Rāyavācakamu*. Honolulu: University of Hawaii Press (1993).

Secondary sources

Aiyangar, S. Krishnaswami. *Ancient India and South Indian History & Culture*. Poona: Oriental Book Agency (1941).

Aiyangar (Ayyangar), S. Krishnaswami. *Sources of Vijayanagara History*. Madras: University of Madras (1919).

Aiyangar, S. Krishnaswami, et al. *Vijayanagara: History and Legacy*. New Delhi: Aryan Books (2000).

Apte, Vaman Shivaram. Revised and enlarged edition of Principal V.S. Apte's *The Practical Sanskrit-English Dictionary*. Poona: Prasad Prakashan (1957–9).

Burgess, Jas. (ed.). *Epigraphia Indica: Volume I*. New Delhi: Archaeological Survey of India (1892, reprint 1983).

Chenchiah, P. *A History of Telugu Literature*. New Delhi: Asian Educational Services (1988).

Dallapiccola, Anna L. (ed.). *Vijayanagara – City and Empire: New Currents of Research*. Stuttgart: Steiner Verlag Wiesbaden GmbH (1985).

Dalrymple, William. *White Mughals*. Gurgaon: Penguin Books (2002).

Desai, Ziyaud-Din A. *A Topographical List of Arabic, Persian, and Urdu Inscriptions of South India*. New Delhi: Indian Council of Historical Research (1989).

Dutt, K. Iswara. 'Telugu Literature under the Vijayanagara Empire,' pp. 53–68 in Aiyangar (2000).

Eaton, Richard M. *A Social History of the Deccan 1300–1761: Eight Indian Lives*. Cambridge: Cambridge University Press (2005).

Eaton, Richard M. '"Kiss My Foot," Said the King: Firearms, Diplomacy and the Battle of Raichur, 1520.' *Modern Asian Studies* 43, 1 (2008).

Gollings, John, John M. Fritz and George Michell. *City of Victory, Vijayanagara: The Medieval Hindu Capital of Southern India*. New York: Aperture (1991).

Habib, Irfan. *Economic History of India, AD 1206–1526: The Period of the Delhi Sultanate and the Vijayanagara Empire*. New Delhi: Tulika Books (2016).

Heifetz, Hank and Velcheru Narayana Rao. *For the Lord of the Animals – Poems from the Telugu: The Kalahastisvara Satakamu of Dhurjati*. Berkeley: University of California Press (1987).

Heras, H. and V.K. Bhandarkar. 'Vijayanagara Empire: A Synthesis of South Indian Culture,' pp. 29–38 in Aiyangar (2000).

Kesava Rao, Bandhakavi. 'The Historical Importance of Parijatapaharanam,' pp. 241–4 in Aiyangar (2000).

Khilnani, S. *Incarnations: A History of India in Fifty Lives*. New York: Farrar, Straus and Giroux (2016).

Kotraiah, C.T.M. *King, Court and Capital: An Anthology of Kannada Literary Sources from the Vijayanagara Period*. New Delhi: American Institute of Indian Studies (2003).

Mack, Alexandra. *Spiritual Journey, Imperial City*. New Delhi: Vedam eBooks (2002).

Narasimhaswami, H.K. (ed.). *South Indian Inscriptions. Volume XVI (Telugu Inscriptions of the Vijayanagara Dynasty)*. New Delhi: Archaeological Survey of India (1972).

Narayana Rao, Velcheru. 'Coconut and Honey: Sanskrit and Telugu in Medieval Andhra.' *Social Scientist* 23, 10/12, pp. 22–40 (1995).

Narayana Rao, Velcheru. *Śiva's Warriors*. Princeton: Princeton University Press (1990).

Narayana Rao, Velcheru and David Shulman. *A Poem at the Right Moment*. Berkeley: University of California Press (1998).

Narayana Rao, Velcheru and David Shulman. *Classical Telugu Poetry: An Anthology*. Berkeley: University of California Press (2002).

Narayana Rao, Velcheru, David Shulman and Sanjay Subrahmanyam. 'A New Imperial Idiom in the Sixteenth Century: Krishnadevaraya and His Political Theory of Vijayanagara.' *South Indian Horizons: Felicitation Volume for François Gros on the Occasion of his 70th Birthday*, edited by Jean-Luc Chevillard, Eva Wilden and A. Murugaiyan. Publications du Département d'Indologie – 94. Pondicherry: Institut Français de Pondichéry; École Française d'Extrême-Orient, pp. 597–625 (2004).

Narayana Rao, Velcheru, David Shulman and Sanjay Subrahmanyam. *Symbols of Substance: Court and State in Nāyaka Period Tamilnadu*. Oxford: Oxford University Press (1992).

Narayana Rao, Velcheru, David Shulman and Sanjay Subrahmanyam. *Textures of Time: Writing History in South India, 1600–1800*. Delhi: Permanent Black (2001).

Pollock, Sheldon. *Forms of Knowledge in Early Modern Asia:*

Explorations in the Intellectual History of India and Tibet, 1500–1800. Durham: Duke University Press (2011).

Pollock, Sheldon. *The Language of the Gods in the World of Men*. Berkeley: University of California Press (2006).

Ramanujan, A.K. *Poems of Love and War*. New York: Columbia University Press (1985).

Rangacharya, V. *A Topographical List of the Inscriptions of the Madras Presidency*. Madras: Government Press (1919).

Rao, C.V. Ramachandra. 'Did Kṛṣṇadevarāya Meet with Discomfiture in His Eastern Campaign Against Pratāparudra Gajapati?' *Proceedings of the Indian History Congress*, Vol. 38, pp. 218–21 (1977).

Rao, M.R. 'Hinduism Under Vijayanagara Kings,' pp. 39–51 in Aiyangar (2000).

Rao, M.R. *Krishnadeva Raya*. New Delhi: India Book House (1971).

Ray, Dipti. *Prataparudradeva: The Last Great Suryvamsi King of Orissa*. New Delhi: Northern Book Centre (2007).

Reddy, P. Bhaskar. 'The Inscriptions of Simhachalam: A Cultural Study.' PhD dissertation. Tirupati: Sri Venkateswara University (1991).

Rubies, Joan-Pau. *Travel and Ethnology in the Renaissance: South India Through European Eyes (1250–1625)*. Cambridge: Cambridge University Press (2000).

Sarma, G.V. Prasada. 'When Sri Krishnadevaraya Visited Simhachalam.' *The Hindu*, 30 March 2016. http://www.thehindu.com/news/national/telangana/when-sri-krishnadevaraya-visited-simhachalam/article8411649.ece

Sastri, K.A. Nilakanta and N. Venkataramanayya. *Further Sources of Vijayanagara History*. Madras: University of Madras (1946).

Sen Gupta, Subhadra. *Hampi: Discover the Splendours of Vijayanagar*. New Delhi: Niyogi Books (2010).

Sewell, Robert. 'The Kings of Vijayanagara, AD 1486–1509.' *Journal of the Royal Asiatic Society of Great Britain and Ireland*, pp. 383–95, July (1915).

Sewell, Robert and S.K. Aiyangar. *The Historical Inscriptions of Southern India*. Madras: University of Madras (1932).

Shulman, David. *More Than Real: A History of Imagination in South India*. Cambridge: Harvard University Press (2012).

Stein, Burton. *Peasant State and Society in Medieval South India*. Oxford: Oxford University Press (1994).

Subrahmanyam, R. *Inscriptions of the Suryavaṁśi Gajapatis of Orissa*. New Delhi: Indian Council of Historical Research (1986).

Subrahmanyam, R. *The Sūryavaṁśi Gajapatis of Orissa*. Waltair: Andhra University (1957).

Talbot, Cynthia. *Pre-colonial India in Practice: Society, Region, and Identity in Medieval Andhra*. Oxford: Oxford University Press (2001).

Venkataramanayya, Nelaturi. *Krishnadevarayalu*. Hyderabad: Andhra Pradesh Government Archaeological Series (1972).

Verghese, A. *Hampi*. New Delhi: Oxford University Press (2002).

Vijayaraghavacharya, V. *Inscriptions of Krishnaraya's Time (From 1509 AD to 1531 AD) Volume III*. Delhi: Sri Satguru Publications (1935).

Wagoner, Phillip B. 'Harihara, Bukka, and the Sultan: The Delhi Sultanate in the Political Imagination of Vijayanagara.' *Beyond Turk and Hindu: Rethinking Religious Identities in Islamicate South Asia*, pp. 300–26 (2000).

Wagoner, Phillip B. '"Sultan Among Hindu Kings": Dress, Titles, and the Islamicization of Hindu Culture at Vijayanagara.' *Journal of Asian Studies* 55, 4, pp. 851–80 (November 1996).

Notes

AM *Āmuktamālyada* of Krishnadevaraya (16th century)
MC *Manucaritramu* of Allasani Peddana (16th century)
PA *Pārijātāpaharaṇamu* of Mukku Timmana (16th century)
RV *Rāyavācakamu* (17th century) in Phillip Wagoner's *Tidings of the King* (1993)
FE Chronicles of Paes and Nunes in Robert Sewell's *Forgotten Empire* (1900)

Rāyavācakamu I.1: Opening verse from the salutation (*avatarika*) of the RV; Ramachandra Rao 1982: 1; RV: 75. All verse translations are mine except where indicated.

Part I

1. Coronation

poetic lines in Sanskrit and medieval Kannada: Hultzsch in Burgess 1892: 361–2. **The slab was installed:** Hultzsch in Burgess 1892: 370–1. **official coronation in early 1510:** Aiyangar 1941: 117–8; Sewell 1915: 394. cf. Aiyangar 1941: 118–20; Sastri and Venkataramanayya 1946: 19 for further discussion of the date. **son was Yayati:** MC I.18–20. Note the omission of Yayati's father, Nahusha. The Hampi inscription includes him as do most other traditional genealogies of the *Chandra-vamsha* (Lunar Lineage). **ancestry back to Yadu:** Hultzsch in Burgess 1892: 362. **good qualities and much fame:** MC I.21. In some Puranic sources Turvasu is described as the cursed son who became king of the Mlecchas in the western kingdom. He is believed to be the forefather of the Yavanas, *i.e.*, the Greeks (Ionians, Aeolians, Achaeans and Dorians) but not the Muslims as the term would later refer to. cf. https://www.wisdomlib.org/definition/turvasu. **many famous kings were born:** Hultzsch in Burgess 1892: 367 and MC I.22. **brought stability to it:** MC I.23. cf. Sistla 2012: 131. **protected the righteous:** MC I.24. **Narasa:** MC I.27–8. cf. Sistla 2012: 134. **The Hampi inscription:** Hultzsch in Burgess 1892: 367. **Tulu country:** cf. Pollock 2011: 74. **shudra background:** Some believe that Narasa Nayaka was from the Balija caste, an umbrella term for many martial and mercantile castes. Talbot argues that the transformation of occupational descriptors to caste-based descriptors happened only in the seventeenth century (Talbot 2001: 86). According to Narayana Rao, et al., 'These left-Sudra groups – often referred to by the cover-title Balija, but also including Boyas, left-hand Gollas, Gavaras, and others – were first mobilised by Krishnadevaraya in the Vijayanagara heyday.' (Narayana Rao, et al. 1992: 10, 74). **The**

inscription continues: Hultzsch in Burgess 1892: 368. Narasa is referred to as Nṛsimha and Tippamba as Tippaji. **the Hampi inscription praises:** MC I.32. Hultzsch in Burgess 1892: 368. **'Whichever of you can pry':** Venkataramanayya 1972: 16. **grasped the dagger:** Venkataramanayya 1972: 16. **gave two commands to Timmarasu:** FE: 314–5. **raised Krishnadevaraya to the Lion Throne of Vijayanagara:** FE: 315. Some accounts relate how Krishnadevaraya's first act as king was to confine his nephew (Viranarasimha's son) and brothers (Achyuta, perhaps others as well) to the imperial fortress of Chandragiri far to the southeast in order to 'prevent dissensions in the kingdom' (FE: 165). This practice of keeping royal family members away from the capital was quite common, and Krishnadevaraya may well have spent some time in this well-provisioned fortress during his own youth. ***Rayavacakamu*:** The RV is a 'unique specimen of Telugu historical prose . . . defies classification in terms of any of the usual historiographical genres' (RV: 3). It is 'a later historiographic representation of those events, anachronistically cast . . . in the form of a diplomatic report of the period' (RV: 8). In that sense RV memorializes the attitudes and concerns of seventeenth-century Nayaka period Madurai more than sixteenth-century Vijayanagara. Wagoner adds, 'There is little evidence of any communally defined Hindu–Muslim antagonism in the Vijayanagara period proper (*i.e.*, up to 1565), the present text provides unmistakable evidence that an anti-Islamic polemic was indeed taking shape in the South by the closing years of the sixteenth century' (RV: 52). **signet ring of the kingdom:** RV: 87. **Also present**: Appaji, along with his son Kondamarasu and his grandson Ayyamarasu. Names given for the official state clerk Rayasam Ramachandrayya and the state treasurer Bokkasam Bhaskarayya. **sixteen great donations and other meritorious acts:** The sixteen great donations or *mahādānas* were large-scale public gifts sponsored by great kings as symbols of their power and generosity. One of them was the famous Tulapurusha rite in which the king donates his weight in gold. cf. Kotraiah 2003: 44. **Lord Vishnu himself:** RV: 87–8. **scented water:** The king put on a pair of wooden sandals and took one hundred steps while reciting the *Shorter Ramayana* (*Saṃkṣipta Rāmāyaṇa*). cf. RV: 88, 128 and 192. **obey his command, whatever it may be:** In the 1962 Telugu film *Mahamantri Timmarasu*, this incident is depicted as taking place in the sabha in front of all the gathered lords and vassals. **young king:** Sadly we have no reliable information about the king's childhood, although some evidence points to his upbringing away from court, perhaps in Penukonda or maybe Chandragiri, both well-established Vijayanagara strongholds that often served as secondary capitals. Often young Vijayanagara princes would be sent to one of these two locations in order to be kept away from machinations at the capital. For example, when Krishnadevaraya ascended the throne, he promptly sent his young nephew to either Penukonda or Chandragiri, almost as a type of house arrest. **proper conduct of a king:** RV: 88. **'king who rises to fill it':** Verse cited in RV, Ramachandra Rao 1982: 13. cf. RV: 89, 192–3. **'harshness in war and wasteful spending':** RV: 89. cf. Notes in RV: 192–3. **'protect the good':** RV: 94. **'dharma':** RV: 56. **reign:** One policy that Krishnadevaraya immediately implemented after being crowned in 1510 was a remittance of a marriage tax 'which had hitherto been enforced on all brides and bridegrooms' (Sewell 1932: 238). **'flow into the treasury':** RV: 94–5. **true treasury of kings:** Verse cited in RV, Ramachandra Rao 1982: 18. cf. RV: 95. **'make your fame shine':** RV: 96. **saying about him:** RV: 96.

2. The Early Days

fast of foot: Spies who were as fast as the wind (*vayu*), others fast as thought (*mano-vega*), Kotraiah 2003: 68. **art of disguise:** RV: 97. **cover of this book:** During one of his pilgrimages to Tirupati Krishnadevaraya 'had a copper image made of himself, with his hands folded in respect and flanked by his queens Tirumaladevi and Chinnadevi, so that he could always remain standing there in the eastern doorway to attend on his lord' (RV: 157); see RV: 216, Note 15 for more information. **smallpox on his face:** FE: 246–7. **enter the great hall:** cf. AM IV.271 and Kotraiah 2003: 51–2. **remain happy and quiet:** RV: 98. **the queen he adored above all others:** FE: 362–3. **king was lord of all:** FE: 135–6. **under Mughal rule:** Noted Vijayanagara historian Burton Stein denies that the administrative unity of south India brought about by Vijayanagara had any particular economic significance. He dismissed the empire as no more than 'an important variant form of segmentary organization'. Habib argues that 'a better case can be made out for a system of territorial tax assignments to nayakas, or military officers, for their own pay and maintenance of their troops, on the lines of the iqta's of the Delhi sultanate . . .' (Habib 2016: 105–6). cf. 'The picture of a centralized administration presented by foreign observes . . . and *Rayavacakamu* is not to be dismissed as unrealistic; it is largely sustained also by epigraphical evidence' (Habib 2016: 106; see also Karashima and Y. Subbarayulu). **forces far and wide:** Verse cited in RV, Ramachandra Rao 1982: 23. cf. RV: 99–100 and *Artha-śāstra* IX.3.10. **'How much revenue':** RV: 100. **'your majesty's consideration':** RV: 100–1. **temple:** Identified as the Pallikonda Ranganathaswami temple. One such temple exists today but deep in Tamil country. **there in secret:** RV: 102. **Krishnadevaraya was waiting:** RV: 102–3. **'firm ground!':** RV: 107. **following close behind:** RV: 103–6. **'minister like Appaji':** RV: 106. **most trusted adviser:** Kotraiah 2003: 37; a Kannada inscription describes the qualities of a good minister, and explicitly mentions that a minister should be brahman, perhaps a vaishya, but never a kshatriya or a shudra. cf. Eighteen types of ministerial posts (Kotraiah 2003: 56); the inscription follows with a description of good ministers (Kotraiah 2003: 37–8) and an ideal minister (Baichappa from *Ramanatha Charite*). cf. AM IV.211, use of individual as exemplar and Kotraiah 2003: 55. **branch of the government:** AM IV.211. **'stars shall shine!':** Vijayaraghavacharya 1935: 96; 'Lakshmi-Ammangar, wife of Pradhani Saluva-Timmaiyyangar, son of Rachcharasar of Kaundinya-gotra and Yajus-sakha' also made a donation (Vijayaraghavacharya 1935: 87–8). **prime minister of the whole kingdom:** Sastri and Venkataramanayya 1946: 135. **influential family:** Ayyangar 1919: 144. **'act as to the king':** FE: 250. **'configuration of political power':** Talbot 2001:

11. **'implementing this policy':** AM IV.207. Interestingly, all the Deccan sultanates retained brahmans in ministerial posts. As William Dalrymple writes, 'Every Muslim sultan in the region made a point of employing a Hindu Chief Minister' (Dalrymple 2002: 26). **'gently on his heart':** AM IV.261: 'A fort should be governed by a brahman who is from a good family, loyal, well educated, righteous and brave. He will stock the citadel with various provisions like sour milk cheese to sustain the people for a long time. He will maintain the treasury and relieve the people's troubles by spending neither too much nor too little. He will give lands to lords, even if they are tiny as ants, but limit their access. He will see to it that the king and his people are without troubles, and that panic runs through his enemies. And after finding that the enemy is weak by means of spies, he would seize their land quickly, like a heron spearing its prey. With a brahman at the head of a fort, the king can rest peacefully, his hand resting gently on his heart.' **'belong to the government':** FE: 245. cf. As Stein and Eaton have discussed: 'Krishna Raya never planted his own kinsmen in central ministries or in the command of major forts. Rather, he continued the earlier practice of hiring large numbers of mercenary troops – Portuguese gunners, Deccani and Western cavalry – and of placing Brahmans, to check, temporarily, the power of quasi-independent generalissimos and to centralize the state to a greater degree than ever before' (Eaton 2005: 90 and Stein 1994: 43).

3. The Medieval Deccan

Until the early fourteenth century: Rao 1971: 3. **penetrate into the south:** FE: 1–2. **rose in power:** Rao 1971: 4. **prisoners to Delhi:** For additional stories and variations of this encounter, see FE: 20–3 and Wagoner 2000. **Hindu kingdom of Vijayanagara:** Kulke 1985: 120; Wagoner 1996: 873. **'religious conversion':** Wagoner 1996: 874. **'measure of expediency':** Rao 1971: 4. **float in the sky:** FE: 243. **'natural fortress':** Verghese 2002: 9. **many holy places:** Verghese 2002: 7. cf. Kotraiah 2003: 23–7. **worshipped in the area for centuries:** Verghese 2002: 6; epigraphical evidence from the seventh century, but worship was surely earlier. **important festivals:** Verghese 2002: 6. **some kind of omen:** FE: 299. **'City of the Hare':** RV: 44. **'he ends up powerless':** RV: 85; for variants of this foundational myth, see RV: 33–50. **'city exists':** RV: 83. **Devagiri in the Deccan:** FE: 14.

4. The Expanding Empire

the Portuguese: In the Portuguese chronicles of Nunes and Paes, the most commonly used name for the empire of Vijayanagara is Narsinga, probably related to the earlier king named Narasimha. In later Portuguese writings the name Bisnaga (a variant of Vijayanagara) became more common. **'destroy the Samorin':** Birch 1877, Commentaries II: 73. **read as follows:** Birch 1877, Commentaries II: 71–3. **'require from his kingdom':** Birch 1877, Commentaries II: 74–5. **was hardly cordial:** An earlier, more amicable encounter between

Viranarasimharaya and a Portuguese minister is recorded as follows: 'On the very day Almeida arrived at the port of Cannanore, Narasingraya's minister went on board the vessel and had an interview with him. This is how it happened: On hearing of the greatness of the victory of the Portuguese, the Raya sent his minister from Anegundi to Cannanore; the minister submitted that "the Raya was willing to enter into a treaty with Emanuel, that he proposed to offer the hand of his daughter to Emanuel's son, and that the necklace of brilliants sent be not refused." The Portuguese were immensely pleased to hear this message as also of the fame and glory of the Raya's kingdom. Therefore the Raya held the Mussalmans in hatred, and ever kept them in check' (Sastri and Venkataramanayya 1946: 86). **'grown prosperous':** Birch 1877, Commentaries II: 95. **'shipped across the Arabian Sea':** Eaton 2005: 60. **'both pay tribute':** Rubies 2000: 191–2, footnote 64. **'Arabia and Persia will win':** Rubies 2000: 191–2, footnote 64. **treated lavishly:** AM IV.258. **enthusiastic reception:** Aiyangar 1941: 128. **Friar Luis was murdered:** FE: 125. **not to commit themselves too far:** Aiyangar 1941: 128. **'prolongation of negotiations':** Rao 1971: 16. **Ummattur, near modern-day Mysore:** Venkataramanayya 1972: 31. **'Our ancestors':** The Gangaraja is claiming that his people are the descendants of Karnataka kings, successors of Hoysalas and Wodeyar princes, and that they once ruled alongside the Konkani Varma kings (Venkataramanayya 1972: 21). **'just one day':** RV: 137. **'for over a year':** Sastri and Venkataramanayya 1946: 100. **Kaveri:** 'pulled down the walls of Ummattur and Sivasamudram'

(Ayyangar 1919: 138). cf. PA II.104 mentions Ummattur and Sivasamudram (Venkataramanayya 1972: 28). **'Lord Adi Ranganayaka':** This may have been Krishnadevaraya's first darshanam of Lord Ranganatha; it may have inspired him to later write about Srirangam in his *Amuktamalyada*. **loyal to him:** Venkataramanayya 1972: 32. **'whole of the south':** Sewell 1932: 236.

5. Bijapur and the Sultans

According to historian R. Subrahmanyam: Subrahmanyam 1957: 98. **'plundered by the victors':** Ferishta III/2.7. **signal of attack:** RV: 137. **'Mahmud Shah':** RV: 210. **Pemmasani Ramalingama Nayadu:** The influential Pemmasani family, who ruled from the southern fort of Gandikota, provided ministers like Pemmasani Timma who served the Aravidus. cf. chatu verse about Ramalinga causing three ministers to bow down (*Further Sources II*, no. 166). **'fight to the finish':** RV: 138. **'waiting bride':** RV: 138. **'six slices to the blow':** RV: 138. **mounted his elephant:** RV: 138. **'ran for the river':** RV: 140. **swirling waters:** RV: 140. **across the river:** An account of the siege of Gulbarga and Krishnadevaraya's care for his men: 'A seasoned warrior chief named Cannama Nayadu of Kadavakolanu presented himself and his men to Krishnadevaraya as he set out to besiege Gulbarga. When the enemy rushed them the king screamed, "If you fight in this battle with the enemy without turning your back on him, and put him to flight, we will award you richly!" And in "the sanguinary battle that followed" the troops fell upon each other and Cannama Nayudu and his men charged into the fray. Eventually the Vijayanagara troops proved victorious and Krishnadevaraya "commanded that the triumphant boar standard should be planted on the battlements of Gulbarga and that the drum of victory should be sounded." And then in a moment that speaks to Krishnadevaraya's compassionate leadership, the king dresses the wounds of his fallen men. "Then Krishnadevaraya causing all his wounded officers to be brought to his presence, enquired into their condition, and ordered the surgeons to dress their wounds. On making enquir[i]es about the condition of old Cannama Nayadu, he was told that the old warrior was lying seriously wounded in some other part of the battlefield. Krishnadevaraya went personally in search of the wounded captain, and causing his wounds to be dressed, had him removed to a tent very near his own, where he carefully tended him until he recovered'" (Sastri and Venkataramanayya 1946: 102–4). There are varying accounts of this battle. Venkataramanayya argues that this battle fits the description of the battle at Devni/Devli/Diwani. cf. *Burhan-i-ma'asir* and *Tarikh-i-Sultan Muhammad Quli Qutb Shahi*, battle occurred 1509/10. cf. *Further Sources* I.189–93 and Venkataramanayya 1972: 44–5. **this victory:** At this great victory, Mukku Timmana, the celebrated Vijayanagara court poet, seems to have been present with the troops. He is said to have spontaneously composed the following verse in praise of his patron's victory: 'Krishnaraya the Man-Lion! You slew the Turks from afar by the mere power of your great name. O Lord of the elephant king! At the mere sight of you, the great host of elephants hurried away in fear!' (RV: 141). **'horse remaining':** RV: 136. **'sounds of our victory':** RV: 137. **'devastating that territory':** RV: 138. **'increased daily in power':** Ferishta III/1.338. **Vanquisher of Sultans:** Rao 1971: 17; some aver that the title was in regard to the defeat of the Bahmani sultan Muhammad Shah. **praise poem:** This verse is placed in the voice of the court's pandits. And unlike most of the other *vamsha-stuti* verses that are taken from Peddana's *Manu Caritramu*, this unique poem seems to have been penned by the king himself. **decapitated head:** AM I.42. cf. MC II.81. Here the king makes direct reference to Edula Khan, or Yusuf Adil Shah, the ageing sultan of Bijapur. Ferishta does not repay this favour in his chronicles for there is scarcely a reference to Krishnadevaraya in his *Tarikh-i-Ferishta*, let alone a specific mention of his name. The effigy mentioned in the translation is not made to be burned; its purpose is to ward off evil spirits. Sistla translates, 'You slaughtered the dreadful Yadul Khan, and hung his head at the entrance so that no evil entered your empire' (Sistla 2010: 153). MC II.81 mentions Kalabarigi (Gulbarga) but oddly in reference to the king of Kataka (*i.e.*, Prataparudradeva). **'imported' to court:** cf. Eaton 2005: 67–9. **'Yusuf Adil Shah's destruction':** Ferishta III/1.302. **'led by example':** Ferishta III/2.18. **Shia Islam:** For some time Ahmadnagar also supported Shia Islam. Bijapur, however, during the reign of Ibrahim Adil Shah I (1534–58) and from Ibrahim Adil Shah II's reign (1580–1627) to the sultanate's demise in 1686, favoured Sunni Islam. **'revolted against him':** Ferishta III/1.337. **'your faith for yourself':** Ferishta III/2.14. The sultan's catholic views are well captured in a story told about one of his successors. 'Guis-ud-Din, a celebrated divine of Persia, much respected for his abilities and purity of life, was once asked by [Yusuf's descendant] Ibrahim Adil Shah, which was the best of all the various sects of Islam? He replied, "Suppose a great monarch is seated in a palace, with many gates leading to it, and through whichever you enter you see the King . . . your business is with the King and not with those at his gate"' (Ferishta III/2.14). Those that followed Yusuf's Shia faith were few but powerful, causing tensions with local Sunnis at the Bijapur court, not to mention continued consternation from the other four sultanates. At some point Yusuf did revert to Sunni Islam (Ferishta III/2.17), albeit for strictly political and not religious reasons. By all accounts, his court and kingdom remained truly tolerant and cosmopolitan. **'ceremonies of the other':** Ferishta III/2.14. **'princely magnificence':** FE: 61. **polarization of these identities:** 'There is little evidence of any communally defined Hindu–Muslim antagonism in the Vijayanagara period proper (*i.e.*, up to 1565), the present text provides unmistakable evidence that an anti-Islamic polemic was indeed taking shape in the South by the closing years of the sixteenth century' (Wagoner 1993: 52). **'killers':** RV: 110. **'Turks':** Throughout RV the word *turakalu* is used to refer to Muslims regardless of ethnic identity. The Portuguese similarly used the word Moors, while Krishnadevaraya preferred Yavanas. In various sources Hindus are referred to as heathens and/or gentiles. In most quotes I have retained idiosyncratic usages, while in prose I have often normalized terms to Hindu and Muslim. **'Kali Age':** RV: 113. **'treacherous**

dispositions': Ferishta III/1/250. **empire's raison d'être:** Aiyangar viewed the foundation of Vijayanagara as a 'great national effort' (Aiyangar 1941: 117). **'two and a half centuries':** FE: 1–2. **oversimplified narrative:** 'Two points seem implicit in such a statement: first, that the historical significance of the Vijayanagara period is as an era of cultural conservatism, during which "classical" forms of Hindu culture were preserved with little alteration and transmitted down to the present; and second, that the culture of South India has remained more authentically and purely "Hindu" than that of North India, where cultural forms and practices – even within a Hindu context – have been greatly altered through a long period of contact and interaction with Islamic forms' (Wagoner 1996: 852). **Western and Indian historians:** Some examples: 'The rise of the Vijayanagara kingdom in the fourteenth century was mainly due to the universal desire felt all over South India among all classes of Hindus to protect their Dharma against the inroads of enemies' (Rao 2000: 39); 'Founded at a time when everything that a Hindu loved and venerated was on the verge of total annihilation, the empire came into existence over the ashes of the southern kingdoms, and represented the Hindu cause, fought for it, and for over three centuries held sway in the South . . . every Hindu state . . . had fallen a prey to the invader's greed for gold' (Heras and Bhandarkar 2000: 29); 'Out of this chaos and insecurity imposed and continued by the Muslim conquest . . . the symbol and focal point of this Hindu revival and resurgence was the famous Vijayanagara Empire' (Rao 1971: 1); 'Two centuries and a half of unremitting resistance to the aggressive Moslem-power . . . repeated blows of the Moslem hammer . . . effort of reconstruction was carried on as a sacred trust' (Aiyangar 1941: 117–8); 'Being an empire founded chiefly for the protection of Dharma, it proved to be the asylum of the much-harassed Hindus who looked upon its rulers as the true representatives of all that was noble in Hindu culture' (Heras and Bhandarkar 2000: 38); and Vijayanagara was the 'savior of Hinduism' (Rao 2000: 40). **'Vijayanagara period':** Wagoner 1996: 852. ***kabayi* (robes):** See Wagoner 1996. **Muslims and Islam:** Wagoner 1996: 855, citing Hodgson 1977: 59. **culture like India's:** 'For South Asianists, however, the distinction is often lost due to the impact of communal ideology with its attendant blurring of the boundaries between religion and politics' (Wagoner 1996: 855). This to me seems natural and inevitable in a society that did not separate religion from public life. Wagoner continues, 'The fact that Islamicization is a process unfolding through the medium of secular culture and, as such, has little to do with religion per se cannot be overstated in the South Asian context. Indeed, failure to recognize the distinction stressed by Hodgson between the Islamic religion and an associated, but distinct and separable, Islamicate civilization lies at the root of many fundamental misunderstandings that continue to hamper interpretation of the history of Vijayanagara, and, one suspects, of medieval South Asia in general' (Wagoner 1996: 872–3). **process of cultural interaction:** Wagoner 1996: 874–5; cf. Ernst 1992: 18–37, Wagoner 1994, Talbot 1995 and Metcalf 1995. **'cow slaughterers':** Ferishta III/1: 194. **lighter tone:** cf. two chatu poems from Peddana mention the war cries of Muslim soldiers as they ascended to heaven, and the sound of Krishnadevaraya's war drums piercing the hearts of the ladies of Bidar (*i.e.*, they knew their husbands were dead!). Even Delhi fortified its gates (Sastri and Venkataramanayya 1946: 101–2); hardships of wives of Gulbarga khans, maliks and vaziers (Sastri and Venkataramanayya 1946: 102); cf. MC I.81 (Gulbarga) and MC III.142 (Yavana) (Sastri and Venkataramanayya 1946: 105–6). **'Saci as bibi':** Sastri and Venkataramanayya 1946: 135. A related image appears in the king's own *Amuktamalyada* when he writes (in the voice of his pandits): 'O Krishna Raya . . . your battle sword slew the swift Yavana lords! They filled Amaravati, the city of heaven, with a raucous uproar as they guzzled down honey-wine from heavenly trees. They grabbed at the singsongy lute players, breaking their strings like taught drawn bows. Whenever they saw Rambha or the other apsaras, they groped at that their full round breasts. And with their boots still on, they stamped out the sand lingas made by the Seven Sages on the banks of the Ganga, while frightened celestial seers licked their fingers to wipe away the ochre that marks their brows' (AM I.41). The conceit here is that frightful brahmans wipe away their religious markings so as not to be detected by the invading Yavanas. Compare this poem to a humorous chatu verse quoted in *Further Sources II* (Sastri and Venkataramanayya 1946: 135). **against each other:** 'Soldiers of Islamic faith [horsemen] were also ready for battle . . .' where a distinction is made between Hindu and non-Hindu warriors (Kotraiah 2003: 69). Also 'on the right was the mass of soldiers of the shudra caste . . .' where caste distinctions are also made (Kotraiah 2003: 69–70).

Part II

6. The Eastern Mountain

'revolt against me still': FE: 316. **'third was Udayagiri':** FE: 308. After Narasimha's death, three fortresses were unable to be taken: Raichur, Udayagiri and Conadolgi (Sewell thinks Kondavidu, maybe also Chandragiri, but not likely). **'against these places':** FE: 316. **thirteenth century:** Perhaps during the rule of Langula Narasinghadeva of the Eastern Gangas, dynastic rulers of Kalinga who preceded the Gajapatis. **set out from Vijayanagara:** Rao 1971: 18; FE: 316; perhaps a later date of 1514 (Aiyangar 1941: 143). **He rallied support:** Subrahmanyam 1957: 100. **He garnered the support:** He even made allegiances with subordinates like Tulu and Boya chiefs (Rao 1971: 21). **overflowing river:** AM IV.247. **cup for offering milk:** Vijayaraghavacharya 1935: 131. **keep perfumes:** Vijayaraghavacharya 1935: 136. **local rulers and merchants:** One merchant, Kondu-setti, gives a village 'which was granted to you by Krishnaraya Maharaya as *umbalikai* (*i.e.*, a Jaghir village granted for certain services rendered by you in connection with the supply of provisions for the army during Krishnaraya's military progress in the south)' (Vijayaraghavacharya 1935: 258). *umbalikai* = rent-free land granted for a service. **enemy to surrender:** For preparations for defence of a fort, see Kotraiah 2003: 74; for a detailed description of a fort siege, see Kotraiah 2003: 74 and FE: 316. **Sridevi and Bhudevi:** Vijayaraghavacharya 1935: 142. **'protect you now':** Vijayaraghavacharya 1935: 149. **Suvarnamukhari river:** The

Sankritized Suvarnamukhari is known locally as the Mogileru river. **'highest truth':** *Kalahasti Shatakamu* CVIII (Heifetz and Rao 1987: 122). ***sri-kala-hasti*:** The Panchamahabhuta Lingas are the Earth linga at Ekambareshwar (Kanchipuram), the Water linga at Jambukeshwar (Thiruvanaikaval), the Fire linga Arunachaleshwar (Thiruvannamalai), the Air linga at Kalahasti and the Space linga at Thillai Natarajar (Cidambaram). **central *gopuram*:** Rao 1971: 36. **'Muslim or Heathen':** Dames 1918: 202. **Tirumala Rautaraya:** Some think the fort commander was Praharesvara Patra, mentioned in AM III.93 at Kondapalli (Subrahmanyam 1957: 100); Tirumala Rautaraya is also mentioned as Tirumalakanta in other sources. **their only ally:** Rao 1971: 21. One report suggests that at this point, Prataparudradeva hastened south to offer his uncle some relief, but that Krishnadevaraya quickly dispatched half his forces to push him back to Kondavidu, the Gajapati's southern headquarters. **'sweet palm liquor':** Paraphrase of excerpt from the *Channabasava Purana* from Kotraiah 2003: 71. **token of submission:** Rao 1971: 22; Narayana Rao and Shulman 2002: 43. **'sparkling at my feet':** AM I.89. **'drag on and on':** AM IV.263. **9 June 1514:** Subrahmanyam 1957: 101; Subrahmanyam 1986: xxiv; Sewell claims the fall of Udayagiri was accomplished some days (perhaps weeks or even a few months) before this date (Sewell 1932: 239). **'could show her':** FE: 317. **Kampanna:** Rao 1971: 23; Vijayaraghavacharya 1935: 173. **new regent:** Subrahmanyam 1957: 101. ***raja-guru* of the king:** Rao 1971: 23. **mandapam in Vijayanagara:** From inscriptions at the Krishnaswami temple in Krishnapuram,

Vijayanagara, we learn that Krishnadevaraya carried away a Balakrishna idol from Udayagiri and installed it in a 'jeweled mandapam' in Krishnapuram on 16 February 1515 (Subrahmanyam 1957: 100). The temple itself was a new construction sponsored by Krishnadevaraya. At the same time, he began building the Hazara Ramaswami temple (FE: 130–1). On earlier temple constructions and donations in Vijayanagara (re: Vitthalaswami temple and Ramachandra temple), see Sewell 1932: 239. Later, in 1516, Krishnadevaraya built a hundred-pillared hall in the Vitthalaswami temple in Vijayanagara, and another such pillared mandapam at Kalahasti (Sewell 1932: 241). **idol from Vijayanagara:** Subrahmanyam 1957: 100; cf. re: Udayagiri (Sistla 2010: 96–8). **'kingdom of the Gajapati':** FE: 317. **all the soldiers:** FE: 317.

7. Tirupati and Temples

social stratification: See the *Maladasari-katha* embedded in the king's *Amuktamalyada* which narrates the tale of an untouchable devotee who redeems a brahman rakshasa and attains ultimate liberation. See Reddy 2014 for a full translation. **temple complex in the world:** As the legend goes, Venkateshwara in his earthly form as the peasant Srinivasa fell in love with the princess Padmavati and took out a loan from Kubera, the Lord of Wealth, in order to afford the royal wedding. The donations offered by pilgrims are believed to help pay off the lord's mounting debt; to this day he is known as *vaddi-kasula-vadu*, the one who continues to pay interest on borrowed money! **'for**

your decoration': Vijayaraghavacharya 1935: 124–5. **Telugu, Tamil and Kannada:** Vijayaraghavacharya 1935: 123. Some inscriptions are in the unique Nandinagari script, a variant of Devanagari used in the Deccan and south India. **'mother tongue':** Vijayaraghavacharya 1935: 123. **generals:** Generous temple gifts made by Periya Obalanayakar Ramanayakar, chief commander for three generations of Vijayanagara kings (Vijayaraghavacharya 1935: 2–3, 101); other nayakas or government officials made donations 'for the merit of Krishnaraya Maharaya', like Udiyam Ellappa Nayakkar who gave three villages (Vijayaraghavacharya 1935: 220). **wealthy women:** Local merchant donations (Vijayaraghavacharya 1935: 13); Dharmapuram Sittamu-setti gave a huge donation (Vijayaraghavacharya 1935: 251); large donation by Tippu-setti, local merchant (Vijayaraghavacharya 1935: 41); also Komattis, headed by Pachchai Lingu-setti, 'belonging to the Komati class of Vaisya caste' (Vijayaraghavacharya 1935: 76). Specific guilds and business groups: 'record on stone in favor of Sabhaiyar (members of the assembly) of Tiruchchukanur (Tiruchanur) belonging to different gotras' at Padmavati temple (Vijayaraghavacharya 1935: 90). Also one Sinnappareddi, son of Surappareddi-Tammureddi of the Mudidar family of the Vellala caste, made a donation on the occasion of a solar eclipse for the merit of Krishnadevaraya (Vijayaraghavacharya 1935: 344). **public works projects:** Vijayaraghavacharya 1935: 6–8. **'various sauces':** Vijayaraghavacharya 1935: 10–11. **amount of prasadam:** Tirumala used Malaikiniyaninran-kal versus Chalukya-narayanan-kal at Tirupati (Vijayaraghavacharya

1935: 11). **minister Timmarasu:** Vijayaraghavacharya 1935: 94. cf. Tirupati Devasthanam Epigraphical Report, pp. 191–5. We learn that he was a brahman and a literary scholar of some renown. 'May the glorious minister Timmana, whose mind is like a bee forever worshipping the lotus feet of Srinivasa, be victorious as long as the moon and stars shed light' (Vijayaraghavacharya 1935: 96). **Narasayya, a doorkeeper:** Narasayya, the palace doorkeeper of Sri-virapratapa Sri-vira Krishnaraya Maharaya, his brother Timmayya and even Tayi Basavamma, bow in eternal devotion to Venkateshwara (Vijayaraghavacharya 1935: 103). **'royal person at all times':** *adaippam* officer = betel bearer of the king. He 'had to be in attendance upon the royal person, just like the *udiyam*'. Continued to serve as adaippam for Achyuta Raya (Vijayaraghavacharya 1935: 282). Donation by adaippam Bhaiyappa-Nayakar, son of Timmappa-Nayakar, for the merit of Krishnaraya Maharaya and Timmappa-Nayakar; also *adiyappan*, 'one of the door-keepers of the king . . . constructed this matham and mandapam' (Vijayaraghavacharya 1935: 346). **ritual priest:** Yajna-Narayana-Bhattar, *purohitar* (court priest) of Krishnadevaraya, accompanied him on the fourth pilgrimage, made charitable donation of 10,000 *nar-pannam* for improving tanks and channels, and food offerings (Vijayaraghavacharya 1935: 192). **personal bodyguard:** 'Baguri Mallarasa, the body-guard of Krishnaraya Maharaya executed this Dharma-sasanam (deed of charity). Sripati, son of Peddayasari, the state engraver and rayasam officer (secretary) of Krishnaraya Maharaya, accompanying the king to Tirumalai engraved this sasanam'. (Vijayaraghavacharya 1935: 182). For Mallarasa 'personal staff of king', see also Vijayaraghavacharya 1935: 273. Perhaps the most detailed donation comes from Karanikka Bhasavarasar, not surprisingly, the king's state accountant. After constructing a tank and donating all the proceeds to the temple 'for the merit of Krishnaraya Maharaya', he built a mandapam and a flower garden, made a huge contribution to the Spring Festival, and made cash donations to several temple workers including reciters of the Vedas, cooks, repairmen, fuel suppliers, servants, basket-makers, devadasis and many others (Vijayaraghavacharya 1935: 217). **Timmarasu's wife:** 'Lakshmi-Ammangar, wife of Pradhani Saluva-Timmaiyyangar, son of Rachcharasar of Kaundinya-gotra and Yajus-sakha . . . The Appayyan, son of Nadindla-Timmaraja and son-in-law to you will be entitled to receive the one nali of prasadam due to the donor' (Vijayaraghavacharya 1935: 87–8). **Vengalamman:** Vijayaraghavacharya 1935: 336. **'Krishnaraya Maharaya':** Vijayaraghavacharya 1935: 270.

8. Kondavidu Fort

governor of Udayagiri: Donation 'in favor of rayasam Kondamarasayyar son of Timmarasayyangar . . . since you have granted Mulumbundi village situated in Nellur-sirmai in the province of Udayagiri'; Kondamarasayyar 'was one of the prominent officers of Krishnaraya who took active part in the battle of Raichur . . . grandson of Sripatyacharya . . . brahmana of Udayagiri-Kannada sect . . . son of Timmarasa-mantri and Sangamambika . . . governor of fortresses like Ghanagiri (Penugonda), Udayagiri and others . . . the hero who actually accomplished for Krishnaraya the planting of the pillars of victory at Simhadri and Srikurmam . . . and a scholar who was acquainted with the curious writings prevalent in the fifty-six countries in India' (Vijayaraghavacharya 1935: 276). **Telugu literary empire:** Narayana Rao and Shulman 2002: 33. **fortresses were centrally administered:** Subrahmanyam 1957: 103. Kondavidu was also the erstwhile Reddy kingdom's capital from where they controlled much of coastal Andhra in the fourteenth and fifteenth centuries. **'snare for three kings':** Subrahmanyam 1957: vii. **one by one:** AM IV.219; cf. variant translation (Narayana Rao, Shulman and Subrahmanyam 2004). **'subjugated the territory':** Rao 1971: 22. **'Gajapati vassals':** Subrahmanyam 1957: 105. Their chief Gannama Nayaka had taken on all the classic titles of a bona fide kshatriya and strengthened the city's hilltop fortress during his governorship under the Gajapati king Purushottama. Vinukonda unceremoniously submitted to Vijayanagara on 23 June 1515 (Sewell 1932: 240). **local agents:** Subrahmanyam 1957: xxv, 106. Another lord named Lakshmipatiraju, however, seems to have remained more loyal to the Gajapatis (at least for a time). He diverted part of his army to Kondavidu in the hope of supporting Prince Virabhadra who was holed up in the citadel. Unfortunately Lakshmipatiraju and his son Srinatharaju would soon have to surrender to Vijayanagara forces. But as was common in those volatile political days, Lakshmipatiraju and Srinatharaju were reinstated in their old positions and continued as loyal officers under Vijayanagara command. **Lord Venkateshwara himself:** This incident likely occurred sometime later, perhaps after the surrender of Prataparudradeva when Krishnadevaraya was returning to Vijayanagara via Vijayawada. **'emanated true compassion':** AM I.11–12. **'for my pleasure':** AM I.13. **king of Karnataka:** AM I.14. **'Telugu is the best':** AM I.15. **central temple spire:** AM I.17. **'truly wonderful':** AM I.17–18. **protect his territories:** Subrahmanyam 1986: xxv. **unidentified coastal river:** Rao 1971: 22; for curious 'salt river' cf. FE: 317. **fled in fear:** 'in which defeat he took many horses and elephants' (FE: 318). **'baffled all invaders':** Subrahmanyam 1957: 107. **'king's strength':** FE: 318. **'capture the fort':** Subrahmanyam 1957: 108, unable to trace the sources. **knocking down their walls:** Inside the fort were Naraharideva, son of Kumara Hamvira, the Gajapati's trusted minister, and Lakshmipatiraju, son of Srinatharaju who would soon pledge allegiance to Vijayanagara. Other Gajapati loyalists inside were Ramaraju, Mallu Khan, Uddanda Khan, Kesava Patra, Balachandra Mahapatra and possibly a queen of the Gajapati (Rao 1971: 23 and Subrahmanyam 1957: 108). See *Epigraphia Indica* and *Record of the Archaeological Survey of India*, Volume 6, Kondavidu inscription. **royal guests:** Subrahmanyam 1986: xxv. Prince Virabhadra was taken prisoner at Kondavidu according to AM and PA, not Kondapalli as Nunes suggests (Subrahmanyam 1957: 113 and Sastri and Venkataramanayya 1946: 113). **'relatives alive':** AM II.101. **Ahobilam and Srisailam:** According to Sewell's reading of Kurnool inscriptions, the king visited Srisailam on 25 July 1515, and Ahobilam on 21 December 1515, most likely on his return journey to the eastern front (Sewell and Aiyangar 1932). **'sword and dagger':** FE: 319. **uncivilized king of Vijayanagara:** FE: 319–20. **the two kings:** There is some historical evidence that Prince Virabhadra did not die at court. Inscriptions reveal that 'pending a permanent solution' Krishnadevaraya made Virabhadra the 'dejure nayaka' of Male-Bennur-Sime from where the prince remitted marriage taxes in 1516 for the merit of his father Prataparudradeva, but in the name of his lord Krishnadevaraya (Subrahmanyam 1986: xxvii). Prince Virabhadra even gifted a tank to the god Tiruvengalanatha of Siri for the merit of Krishnadevaraya (Subrahmanyam 1957: 114). Subrahmanyam qualifies these actions by adding that the donations and titles were all in name only. Virabhadra was given no real freedom or independence, and he was probably kept under house arrest in the luxurious confines of Vijayanagara (Subrahmanyam 1957: 115). **heavenly capital:** AM I.37. One double meaning here is that Indra's celestial capital of Amaravati (*bala-sūdana vīḍu*) refers to Rajamahendravaram, city of the Great Lord of Kings (modern-day Rajahmundry). Vedam Venkataraya Sastry adds that the women (*kāminulu*) mentioned could refer to tribal women in the area (Sastry 1927: 39–40). Srinivas Sistla offers a more audacious reading by interpreting (*bala-sūdana vīḍu*) as an actual town in Kalinga and the women as prostitutes. His translation of the full verse reads: 'Surprising indeed! O Krishna Raya, the lord of all kings! In the past, it seems, the rulers of Kondavidu dug a tunnel to Balasudana-veedu, through which they fled the place! Now, apparently, the freshly wounded Utkala kings and Patra ministers fled from Kondaveedu through the same tunnel to take up jobs as watchmen at whorehouses!' (Sistla 2010: 148–9). Unlike other verses in this section, AM I.37 does not appear in Peddana's MC, nor in Timmana's PA. **'no reason for expecting him':** FE: 318. **'everything in sight':** RV: 144. **stiff resistance:** FE: 318–9 and Rao 1971: 23. Re: Kondapalli, cf. long inscription at Conjeevaram, FE: 131. **intense effort:** AM III.93. **fort in Andhra:** Subrahmanyam 1986: xxvi. **prickly weeds:** RV: 145; the idea is that 'castor beans and swallowworts' are invasive weeds that render the soil barren. **Praharesvara Patra:** Praharesvara Patra = Praharaju Sirascandra Mahapatra (Subrahmanyam 1986: xxvi); cf. AM III.93. **Bijili Khan:** Subrahmanyam 1957: 110. Bijili Khan was either in the Gajapati's employ, or probably, a subordinate of the Qutb Shahi sultan of Golconda, dispatched by his master to defend Kondapalli. **'dusty red earth':** The Gajapati mentioned here is Virarudra, most likely a reference to Prataparudradeva's son. 'People manning the smaller forts there beheld the army advancing on them like the ocean pounding at the shore, and, when they saw the great clouds of dust rising up from the soldiers' feet and eclipsing the rays of the sun, they ran out of their forts in terror' (RV: 143). **royal personage:** Subrahmanyam 1986: xxvi. **'time for reconciliation':** AM IV.267. **toppling dominoes:** Capitulating forts included Anantagiri, Undrakonda, Urlakonda, Aruvapalli, Jallipalli, Kandikonda, Kappalavayi, Nalagonda, Kambhammettu, Kanakagiri, Shankaragiri and others (Subrahmanyam 1986: xxvi). Rao 1971: 24 says the forts were taken by Krishnadevaraya.

9. Rival Kings

'master of the eastern half of Telangana': Rao 1971: 24. **Citap Khan was either:** Subrahmanyam 1986: xxvi. **'Ekasilapuri (Warangal)':** Subrahmanyam 1986: 175. **new political ties:** Subrahmanyam 1957: 122. **borders of his realm:** It was around this time that the Portuguese chronicles tell us of an encounter between Timmarasu and a Mohammedan named Madarmeluquo who commanded a force of 60,000 men. I believe this Madarmeluquo to be the same Citap Khan. He was reported to be a captain of Elrey Daquem. This may be 'the king on this side' or 'the king of the Dakhan', but in any case, the reference is probably to the forces of Sultan Quli Qutb Shah of Golconda (FE: 322). cf. Mohammedan account of affairs at this time (FE: 132–5). **routed his forces:** Chitapu (Citap) Khan 'ambushed them with sixty thousand mounted archers, letting loose a storm of arrows that fell like a monsoon cloudburst on the horsemen and foot soldiers in the passes'. There was confusion in the Vijayanagara ranks but a small force of the best salaried horseman ascended to attack from the rear. Chitapu Khan's small numbers could not defend and they finally retreated and fled, driving them back to their fort (RV: 145–6). **stores of jewels:** FE: 322 and Rao 1971: 35. **righteous Hindu king:** RV gives a detailed description of the Gajapati's daily routine, very similar to Krishnadevaraya's regimen, cf. AM IV.271. **light the evening lamps:** Narayana Rao and Shulman 1998: 130–1. **'low-caste peasant at that':** Narayana Rao 1995: 25. **royal Lunar Lineage:** The 1962

Telugu film *Mahamantri Timmarasu* vividly portrays this social dynamic. **Sri Vaishnava:** Producing such an expansive work like *Amuktamalyada*, steeped as it is in Sri Vaishnava theology, required not only a masterly command of poetics and composition, but an intimate knowledge of Sri Vaishnava arcana. Although Krishnadevaraya was non-sectarian both personally and publicly, a reading of *Amuktamalyada* reveals a man with a deep and sustained personal devotion to the Sri Vaishnava faith. He was likely initiated into the *sampradaya* (tradition) in his youth, and circumstantial evidence suggests that he spent his childhood in the secluded Sri Vaishnava *matham* at Ahobilam (Andhra Pradesh) in the densely forested hills of the Nallamalla range, but no hard proof exists. Some say that a watchful Timmarasu sent Krishnadevaraya away for monastic studies in his childhood in order to shield him from the treacheries at court. Whatever the case may be, the king's magnum opus makes it clear that he was a talented poet as well as a devout Sri Vaishnava. See Sistla (2010: 46–9) for an allegorical interpretation of the text and Krishnadevaraya's connection to various Vaishnava mathams. **'a living Krishna':** AM I.44. **history of Vijayanagara had crystallized:** Narayana Rao and Shulman 2002: 166 and Narayana Rao 1995. **'Gajapati's troops of elephant':** Rao 1971: 15. **about Krishnadevaraya:** Subrahmanyam 1957: 98. **'threw himself on his mercy':** Subrahmanyam 1957: 178. **Establisher of Yavana Rule:** cf. Eaton 2005: 90. **'realized form of kingliness':** Pollock 2006: 15, 166. **Andhra Bhoja:** cf. MCV.105 where the poet laureate Peddana directly compares Krishnadevaraya to the semi-historical King Bhoja. **'fields of war and letters':** *sāhitī-samarāṅgaṇa sārvabhauma* (AM I.44). **'conversant in music and literature':** Prataparudradeva = *nava-koti-karnata-kalubarigesvara*, 'avatara of Jagannatha', *sangita-sahitya sallāpa* = 'conversant in music and literature' (Subrahmanyam 1986: 193). **writing in a vernacular:** Kapilendra and Purushottama 'positively discouraged Telugu in their zeal for Sanskrit'. Contrast this with the treatment of Srinatha, poet laureate of the Reddi kings (Subrahmanyam 1957: 5). **Sanskrit literary tradition:** AM I.13 reads: 'You composed the Story of Madalasa and the Pleasures of Satyabhama and delighted connoisseurs with your natural usage of hyperbole, metaphor, subtle suggestion and sarcasm. You selected the best episodes from the Vedas and the Puranas and compiled the Abridged Essence of All Stories. With great poetic skill you wrote the Jewel of Wisdom that could dispel the sins of any listener, and your Handbook on Aesthetics was praised by scholars for its sweet poetry. All of these works you wrote in Sanskrit, but is it impossible to compose poetry in Telugu? Create a great poem in Telugu for my pleasure!' The texts referred to in this poem are most probably descriptive titles. They are cited in the verse as: *Madālasa-caritra, Satyāvadhū-prīṇanambu, Sakala-kathā-sāra-saṅgrahambu, Jñana-cintāmaṇi* and *Rasa-mañjarī*. **'laws of the Hindus':** Subrahmanyam 1957: 177. **Lolla Lakshmidhara Pandita:** Of note is the fact that after Prataparudradeva's defeat, Lakshmidhara Pandit migrated to the Vijayanagara court. So did another reputed poet Divakara, a specialist in *vyakarana* who illustrated grammatical rules while narrating the story of the Pandavas. Perhaps these court poets were part of Krishnadevaraya's wedding dowry, but more likely they simply found fresh employment with a powerful, new patron (Subrahmanyam 1957: 153). Prataparudra's court of poets and scholars included the famous Vasudeva Sarvabhauma, master of the Navya-Nyaya school of philosophy. He was 'looked upon as the universal referee in Orissa specially on points of law, ritual, philosophy and religion' (Subrahmanyam 1957: 151). **'attempted anything like it':** Narayana Rao and Shulman 2002: 167. **sixteenth-century governance:** See Narayana Rao, Shulman and Subrahmanyam 2004. **literary works to his credit:** Subrahmanyam 1957: 148.

10. The Lion Mountain

main deity: Reddy 1991: 19 and Sarma 2016. 'Three years later, he gifted to the god five villages in the Kalinga-dandapati which was taken from the Gajapati' (Rao 1971: 36). **Gajapati gave no reply:** FE: 319. **'of his own accord':** AM IV. 251. **sultan of Bengal:** Subrahmanyam 1986: xxiv. **'shoe the horses of Vijayanagara':** FE: 319. **mention of this event:** cf. MC I.37 and MC I.39. **famous pillar:** I have not been able to identify this pillar but local residents of Simhachalam assure me that it exists. They also claim that an Ashokan pillar from the third century BC still stands as a marker of that king's famous victory over the Kalingas. **'the blessed King Krishnaraya':** AM IV.289. **Sri Krishnaraya Lord of Men:** Koteswara Rao 2001: 467. **great vassals:** For the names of all sixteen mahapatras, see RV: 147. ***bheda* (dissension):** cf. AM II.39. The 'six traits of a mighty monarch' (*sāḍ-guṇyamu*) are skills related to *sandhi* (peacemaking), *vigraha* (war), *yāna* (invasion), *āsana* (patience), *dvi-dvaya-upāya* (weighing pros and cons) and *samāśraya* (protection). The 'four modes of governance' (*dvi-dvaya-upāya*, literally 'the two pairs of means') are *sāma* (peaceful negotiation) and *dāna* (gift giving) which are considered *sātvika*; and *bheda* (sowing dissension among the enemy) and *daṇḍa* (punishment) which are *rājasika*. There is said to be a pair of *tāmasika* means but this king apparently never resorts to them. **support structure:** Subrahmanyam 1957: 110. **'priceless jewels':** RV: 152. **capital of Cuttack:** Rao 1971: 25. **traitorous lords:** It is noteworthy that the Gajapati, in line with kshatriya tradition, primarily appointed princes and other men of royal blood to important governing positions. Many of the mahapatras were thus Prataparudradeva's own relatives, and so it seems that blood was not thicker than water. Interestingly, this nepotistic practice was in sharp contrast to Krishnadevaraya's policy of keeping local allies in power and appointing loyal brahmans as governors. **'even Cuttack is ours':** '*Orugallu manadi! Kondapalli manadi! Kadani vaduku, vaste Katakam daka manadera!*' Rao 1971: 25. cf. The song of a washerman whose home was ritually blessed by Krishnadevaraya before he set out on the Gajapati campaign (Sastri and Venkataramanayya 1946: 112). **former royal attire:** AM I.39. **siege of Catuir:** Some scholars believe that the city of 'Catuir' as recorded by Nunes is the Gajapati capital Cuttack, while others identify it with Sivasamudram, the citadel of the Gangaraja of Ummattur (cf. FE: 321–2). **reached**

the city gates: FE: 321. **'slaughtering them all':** FE: 321. **'those who wanted to leave':** Rao 1971: 25. **giving each his just due:** FE: 322. **would never recover:** By some accounts, the city of Cuttack was burned in order to force Prataparudradeva into submission (Subrahmanyam 1957: 116). **further devastation:** Subrahmanyam 1986: xxvii. **'I leave for the Gajapati':** RV: 155. **restored to Prataparudradeva:** Though the Gajapati empire was crumbling, Kondapalli would continue to serve as the 'seat of southern viceroyalty of the Orissa kingdom' (Subrahmanyam 1986: xxvii). **'between you and me':** RV: 155. **contrived marriage:** After the Gajapati defeat, Krishnadevaraya donated several villages to the Simhachalam temple complex in August 1519; these villages were likely part of his wedding dowry (Subrahmanyam 1957: 118). **Annapurna:** cf. Sistla 2010: 87–8; cf. *Biographies of Telugu Poets* by Gurujada Sriramamoorthy. **'this side for himself':** FE: 319–20. **'tact of his minister Timmarasu':** Subrahmanyam 1957: 121. **woman of noble birth like herself:** Subrahmanyam 1957: 121. **large water reservoir:** Subrahmanyam 1957: 121. **Qutb Shahi sultanate of Golconda:** By 1520 when Krishnadevaraya was busy battling Bijapur, Quli Qutb Shah had seized the weakened territories of the Gajapati, first taking on the Raya Sitapati of Kambhammettu who rode out to meet him in battle but was defeated (Subrahmanyam 1957: 123). Interestingly, the Persian historian Ferishta's account of the Gajapati campaign years claims that the hill forts of Kondavidu and others were in Mohammedan hands, likely Sultan Quli Qutb Shah of Golconda (FE: 132–4). Ferishta, like all Orissan sources, never mentions Krishnadevaraya by name. **out of shame and fear:** Subrahmanyam 1957: 124. **Krishnaraya's mighty arms:** MC I.37; cf. AM I.36 almost identical to MC I.37. PA I.23 summarizes the battles in verse, including mention of Vinukonda, Bellamukonda, Devarakonda, Anantagiri and Kambhammettu; see also Rao 1971: 25. **Golconda forces:** On his way to Kondavidu, Timmarasu encountered a Mohammedan named Madarmeluquo/Citap Khan (FE: 322); cf. the account given above in reference to Elrey Daquem. Timmarasu with his 2,00,000 men had 'very little fear' . . . he engaged and defeated Madarmeluquo, took him prisoner along with his wife, sons, horses, elephants, much money and stores of jewels . . . all of which he sent back to the capital. According to Nunes, the king put all the captives in prison where they all died (FE: 322). **'the principal person in the kingdom':** FE: 322.

Part III

11. Court of Culture

'thought fabulous': FE: 256–8. **'people one to another':** Dames 1918: 202. **'will endure forever':** RV: 160. **handsome cloths:** FE: 263–4. ***ashta-dig-gajas*:** One formulation of the eight great poets and their major works: Allasani Peddana (*Manu Caritramu*), Nandi Timmana (*Parijata Apaharanamu*), Madayyagari Mallana (*Rajasekhara Caritramu*), Dhurjati (*Sri Kalahasti Mahatmyamu* and *Sri Kalahastisvara Satakamu*), Ayyalaraju Ramabhadra (*Rama Abhyudayamu*), Pingali

Suranna (*Kalapurnodayamu* and *Raghava Pandaviyamu*), Ramarajabhusana (*Vasu Caritramu*) and Tenali Ramakrishna (*Panduranga Mahatmyamu*). It is unlikely that all of these poets graced the Bhuvana Vijayam during Krishnadevaraya's reign, but the importance of their memorialization is that it crystallized a Telugu literary canon and gave shape to a new literary history. **grandsire of Telugu poetry:** MC I.15. **metaphysics and more:** MC I.12–3; cf. Portrait of the king sitting on the throne (Kotraiah 2003: 39) with various female attendants (Kotraiah 2003: 40), description of the court and ranks of those present (Kotraiah 2003: 40), also the evening public audience (Kotraiah 2003: 41). **realm of lyrical poetry:** It was during the reign of the Tuluva dynasty kings that Telugu literature took a 'romantic turn', evolving from an age of 'translating' known Sanskrit texts to an age of innovation when poets created novel stories with fresh expressions. It was a shift 'from religion to romance, from imitation to imagination, from narration to description, and from ethics to aesthetics; Telugu literature assumed a new shape and was completely metamorphosed' (Dutt 2000: 56). **'fields of war and letters':** AM I.44. His other titles include: *kavya-nataka-alankara-marma-jna*, Knower of the Secrets of Poetry, Dance and Aesthetics, and *kavita-pravinya-phanisa*, Lord Sesha of Poetic Skill. **Vasantotsavam:** Vasantotsava (Kotraiah 2003: 87–8), Spring puja description, coloured water, Holi-esque; swings and merry-go-rounds (Kotraiah 2003: 87). **'with his charm':** PA I.139; Krishnadevaraya as 'hearing, along with his queens, the works composed by the poets assembled at his court for the spring festival every year'

(Ayyangar 1919: 138). **'Chaitra Spring festival':** Ayyangar 1919: 142. **sculpture and painting:** The king sponsored the production of various genres of literature from scientific texts and philosophical works to devotional poetry and songs. One particular area that flourished during Vijayanagara times was the theory and practice of *sangita-shastra* or musicology. This was the time of Purandaradasa and Kanakadasa, foundational figures in the history of Carnatic music. And also the age of what came to be known later as the Vijayanagara musical nonet, or the *sangita-shastra nava-ratna*, nine gems of musicology. One of these scholar-practitioners was Krishnadevaraya's court musician Bandaru Lakshminarayana who oversaw the training of all court dancers. His master work was the *Sangitasuryodaya* in Sanskrit (Rao 1971: 44). Tradition even tells us that Krishnadevaraya was himself a talented musician, celebrated for his skills on the veena and his deft accompaniment of dance performances. **even his descendants:** cf. MC I.14. **Peddana his friend:** MC I.15. **mutual respect:** Peddana was the only poet to be awarded the famed *ganda-penderamu*, a precious metal anklet worn by conquering kings and master poets. Here is how he remembered his friend the king: 'Whenever he saw me while riding atop his royal elephant, he would stop, reach out his hand, and lift me up to his side. He gave me whatever I asked for. And on the day he accepted my *Manu Caritramu*, he himself carried my palanquin as we made our way through the city. He declared that I was the only one worthy of the great anklet that honours the best poets, and he clasped it around my foot with his own hand. He called me, Allasani Peddana, the King of Poets, and the Grandsire of Telugu poetry!' Chatu verse; cf. Narayana Rao and Shulman 2002: 157. According to Dutt, Peddana's 'influence in the court was so great, and the esteem of the Emperor for him was so enormous, that Krishnadevaraya took the poet along with him on his Kalinga campaign . . . he was made poet laureate and also appointed as a provincial subordinate by the Emperor' (Dutt 2000: 56). This may be exaggerated but certainly Peddana had the ear of the king and was influential at court outside of literary circles. **Nandi Timmana:** He is also known by the name Mukku Timman on account of a chatu verse famous for the prevalence of nasal sounds; cf. Narayana Rao and Shulman 2002: 178. **Tamil country:** Son of Nandi Singamatya and Tippamba; his spiritual guru was Aghora Shivacharya, from a lineage which traces back to Chidambaram and the Shaiva Siddhanta philosophy/ritual practice of the Tamil south (Kesava Rao 2000: 241). **multilingual poet:** Krishnadevaraya is said to have commissioned Timmana to complete the unfinished *Kannada Bharata* of Kumaravyasa (Kotraiah 2003: 106). Timmana was thus a skilled poet in Kannada and garnered the title *karnataka-kavisarvabhauma* (Rao 1971: 43). **dedicated to the king:** Timmana dedicated PA to Krishnadevaraya; pleased with his 'poetic talent and diction' the king gifted him an *agraharam* (Kesava Rao 2000: 241). **'parijata tree just for you!':** Paraphrase based on Narayana Rao and Shulman 2002: 189. **Tulapurusha rite:** Ayyangar 1919: 138–9 and Kesava Rao 2000: 241; while at Kondavidu, Krishnadevaraya 'visited Amaravati on the Krishna River, weighed himself against gold, and made some munificent gifts to the temple of Amareshvara. Two inscriptions mention this and mention his queens' (Sewell 1932: 240). **weight in gold:** See the classic 1966 Telugu film *Sri Krishna Tulabharam* for a depiction of this story, including a poignant portrayal of Rukmini's love and the power of bhakti. **officers and city governors:** FE: 249–50. **good night's rest:** AM IV.271. **balanced day:** A Kannada prose text known as the *Sri Krishnadevarayana Dinachari* by Timmaya and Mallaya purports to be Krishnadevaraya's diary but 'recent scholarship suggests the possibility that it may be a translation into Kannada of the Telugu *Rayavacakamu*, composed either in the late sixteenth or early seventeenth century at the Nayaka court of Madurai' (Kotraiah 2003: xv). **culture of his court:** Many people at court emulated the king's love and patronage of literary arts. Timmarasu, for example, wrote a respected commentary on Agastya's *Champu Bharata* (Ayyangar 1919: 143). His nephew, Nadindla Gopa, a key figure in the Vijayanagara administration who was granted governorship over Kondavidu, is said to have written *Krishnarjuna Samvadam*, a Telugu work in the folk *dvipada* metre, along with a Sanskrit commentary on the *Prabodha Chandrodaya* of Krishna Mishra. Krishnadevaraya's daughter Mohanangi is remembered as a skilled poet. She supported various poets as a royal patron and even composed her own Telugu work entitled *Marichi Parinayamu*. cf. The story of Mohanangi buying verses from the penniless Narasimhakavi who had been blocked from coming to court by a jealous Peddana (Chenchiah 1998: 76–7).

12. Road to Raichur

Mudgal: We have no clear evidence in regard to how or when Krishnadevaraya was able to reclaim Mudgal, but it most probably occurred during the Gajapati campaign. **'how to break it':** FE: 323; Nunes actually records an exaggerated 'forty years' of peace. **'break the peace':** FE: 323. **confidant of the king:** FE: 323. Cide is likely a rendering of Siddi, a large community of East Africans who found employment in the service of many Deccan kingdoms. **fellow Muslims:** 'Some say that the Adil Shah wrote to him a letter as soon as he got there' (FE: 324). **immediate extradition:** FE: 324. **'many suggestions were made':** FE: 324. **'related to Muhammad':** FE: 324; the reference is unclear but probably implies that Cide Mercar was a sayyid claiming descent from Muhammad. **whereabouts or intentions:** FE: 324. **'honesty in a Moor':** FE: 324–5. **double agent Cide Mercar:** The following is Barros's account of the Cide Mercar affair: 'Crisnarao [Krishnaraya], knowing that he could catch the Hidalcao [Adil Shah] in this trap, called a Moor by name Cide Mercar . . . Crisnarao wrote letters to our Captain . . . on purpose so that the affair might become widely known to all. Cide Mercar, either tempted by the large sum of money in his charge, or swayed by a letter which they say was sent to him by the Hidalcao . . . fled to the Hidalcao from there. The Hidalcao as soon as he arrived sent him to Chaul, saying that he bestowed on him this tanadaria as he was an honourable man of the family of Mahamed . . . ; but in a few days he disappeared from there, and they say that the king ordered his murder after he had taken from him the forty thousand pardaos' (FE: 325). **as they were able:** 'As to the Zemelluco [Nizam Shah] . . . he could find no excuse for not sending some troops to the aid of his sister who was wedded to the Adil Shah' (FE: 325–6). **transcend religious affiliations:** This is not to say that religious identity played no role in the political imagination of the time. Here is one excerpt from Nunes in which his own Lusocentric views on the Moors and their infighting is highlighted: '. . . because the Adil Shah was hated by them all [the other sultans] as being a more powerful chief than they, (for there is little faith amongst the Moors, and they bite one another like dogs and like to see one after the other destroyed)' (FE: 326). **hundreds of war elephants:** See FE: 327 for a detailed, albeit surely inflated, estimate of Krishnadevaraya's forces. **'pick of all his kingdom':** FE: 327. **'number into the field':** Aiyangar 1941: 160. **'needed for his people':** FE: 329. **'everything out here':** FE: 333. **'brush-wood and thorns':** FE: 329. **just for washermen:** FE: 332. **'city of Vijayanagara':** FE: 332. **scouts and water boys:** FE: 328. **'and other things':** FE: 333. **'in a prosperous city':** FE: 333. See also the layout of a camp: 'main and secondary streets . . . this beautiful town built in such a short time, looked like a work of magic'; king's tent in the centre of camp, richly decorated; provisions in the camp: food, weapons, drinks, drugs, etc.; description of army on the move, military entourage: bullock carts, slaves, gear, food, merchants, blacksmiths, artists, non-vegetarian food, intoxicants, etc. (Kotraiah 2003: 70–1). **breast upon the earth:** FE: 331; the conceit was also popular among

Indian poets, cf. Kalidasa's *Meghadutam* I.18. **'of gods, not men':** Eaton 2008: 292. **'an outer moat':** Eaton 2008: 293. **'spoken from one to the other':** FE: 331–2. **twenty elephants:** FE: 331. **last for five years:** FE: 331. **'did great damage':** FE: 331. **'not to mention small ones':** FE: 331–2. **before the Europeans had:** In the course of their Deccan campaigns, 'Ala al-Din Khalaji and Muhammad bin Tughluq had brought with them new siege technology, including extensive groundworks, earthen battlements (*pashib*), mines, wooden siege towers, mangonels, and counterweight trebuchets. The Tughluqs, especially, were great fort builders. At sites like Tughluqabad, in Delhi, one sees their distinctive architectural features: massive projecting buttresses, merlons, turrets, and crenellations. Such features quickly diffused to the Deccan, as at Daulatabad, where ramparts were replaced with a double line in lime-mortar masonry, round bastions, and turrets. The Bahmani rulers continued these traditions in such major forts as Gulbarga, Firuzabad, and Bidar. Gommans, *Mughal Warfare,* pp. 141–4' (Eaton 2008: 293). **'matchlock firearms':** Matchlock firearms are hand-held rifles with a lock in which a wick is placed to ignite the gunpowder (Eaton 2008: 289). **'diplomatic history of the Deccan':** Eaton 2008: 309. **time was right to advance:** FE: 329. **crashing down on him:** FE: 333–4. **birth of time itself:** RV: 143, Wagoner's translation of a verse referring to the Gajapati campaign. **cannons of his own:** Eaton 2008: 301. 'All of this suggests that by 1520 cannon were being used in the field – extensively by Bijapur, at best minimally by Vijayanagara – but with only limited effect' (Eaton 2008: 303). **closest to the**

base: Eaton 2008: 304. **'lay the city open':** FE: 330. **'terror of death':** FE: 330. **150 elephants:** FE: 335–6. **seized control of the ferries:** Eaton 2008: 300.

13. Battle on the Krishna

'patron's own forebear': Eaton 2008: 299–300. **grain of alternative records:** The chronicles of the two Portuguese horse-traders (Paes and Nunes) must be read in the context of their circumstances. Eaton argues that Nunes 'would not seem to have had any motive either to celebrate or to criticize the king' (Eaton 2008: 308), but I would disagree. As Christovão de Figueiredo is reported to have said, the 'whole business of Portuguese was war' (FE: 343), which included the lucrative trade in warhorses. Joan-Pau Rubies speculates that 'the insight and perhaps also the bitterness bred of three years trying unsuccessfully to prosper by selling horses, leads [Nunes] towards an image in which the pretensions of ideal kingship, although not completely obliterated, are nevertheless reduced to human proportions' (Rubies 200: 268; Eaton 2008: 308). Whatever the case, it is clear that the Portuguese merchant chroniclers had a specific set of perspectives that coloured their documentation of Vijayanagara and its people. **no Hindu memory:** 'No epigraphic mention of the battle of Raichur except the solitary record in Tirukkadaiyur where a Brahman named Apatsahaya who carried out some repairs to the Shiva temple there states that he took part in the battle of Raichur. Nor are there any references in literature . . .' (Aiyangar 1941:

151). **a Friday evening no less:** Based on Sewell's extensive calculations, the date of the battle was Saturday, 19 May 1520. cf. Krishnadevaraya 'ordered all to arm themselves at dawn, as he intended then to give battle to the enemy; but the men of the Council said that that day was an unlucky day, and begged him not to attack, as it was a Friday, and they asked him not to attack till Saturday, which they hold for a lucky day' (FE: 336–7). **'pleasures of music and wine':** Ferishta III/2: 29–30. **'attack right then and there':** Eaton 2008: 300. **'two hundred and fifty elephants':** Ferishta III/2: 29–30. **unsuspecting enemy:** FE: 334. **'fault of the wine':** Eaton 2008: 301. **bloody encounter:** FE: 335–6. **king's father-in-law too:** FE: 336. **troops began to flee:** FE: 338. **'Traitors':** The king mounted his horse and moved forward with all his divisions, 'commanding to slay without mercy every man who had fled' (FE: 339). **'Who ranges himself with me':** Based on the account and quotes provided by Nunes (FE: 338–9). **'killed countless more':** FE: 339. **eventually put to flight:** Ferishta III/2: 29–30. **'currents of the Krishna river':** Eaton 2008: 300–1. **each withdrew his forces:** FE: 339–40. **'new and better strategy':** Based on the account and quotes provided by Nunes (FE: 340). **'king ordered to be released':** FE: 342–3. **helped him escape:** FE: 340–1. **Portuguese renegades:** The use of the term *renegados* here is important as it speaks to an increasing number of Portuguese individuals in India who had abandoned imperial service and set out on their own in pursuit of personal glory and wealth (FE: 139, 34). **finally taken hostage:** FE: 342. **as he had done before:** FE: 343. **close to his own quarters:** FE:

343. **trenches near the wall:** FE: 343. **dismantling the fort wall:** FE: 343–4. **gun-making engineers of Goa:** Eaton 2008: 299. There was by this point a bustling munitions plant in Goa from where the Portuguese introduced such new forms of gunpowder technology into the Deccan (Eaton 2008: 296). **firearms in the Deccan:** Eaton 2008: 310, 299. **'entered the city':** FE: 343–4. **approach the citadel unharassed:** FE: 344. **'send in troops':** AM IV.264. **pickaxes and crowbars:** FE: 344. **fired the fatal blow:** FE: 344–5. **'pity and benevolence':** FE: 346. **'enter it tomorrow':** FE: 346. Nunes's detailed account of Raichur provides much insight into the personality and nature of the king; he was fearless, wise and merciful. Take, for example, the treatment of the conquered peasantry where the king's benevolence is noteworthy. cf. Krishnadevaraya's policy of mercy (AM IV.235). **feasting and rejoicing:** FE: 346. **'savior after so many years':** FE: 347. **'soak your own in water':** FE: 348. **feasts and much entertainment:** FE: 349.

14. City and Palace

'deprived of such resources': AM IV.258. **other things to eat:** FE: 252. **'king of Portugal kept up':** FE: 252–3. **'one of his own people':** FE: 251. **'enough of looking at us':** FE: 251. **'day of the week':** AM IV.283. **war helmet from his native Iberia:** Paes seems to be describing an ornamental turban, the shape of which reminded him of a war helmet from Galicia in north-western Iberia. For an in-depth analysis of the Islamicization of Vijayanagara court attire, specifically the *kullayi* (headdress) and *kabayi* (robes), see Wagoner 1996. **'bare feet':** FE: 251–2. **'perfect is he in all things':** FE: 247. **cap in the same fashion as his own:** For more detailed information see Wagoner 1996. **'friendship and love':** Based on Paes (FE: 252). **'no one ever sees':** FE: 284. **'during the feasts':** FE: 284. **'my senses lost!':** FE: 278. **treasury of one of the former kings:** cf. 'Previous kings of this palace for many years past have held it a custom to maintain a treasury . . . locked and sealed, nor opened except when the kings have great need . . . This king has made his treasury different from those of the previous kings, and he puts in it every year ten million pardaos, without taking from them one pardao more than for the expenses of his house' (FE: 282). **women to be trained in dance:** cf. Vijayanagara known as Vardhanavati, painted walls, 'handsome men and beautiful women in various postures and expressions'. cf. Description of diverse audience, orchestra, singing, dance master and his two daughters skilled in sixteen kalas, tambura player, stage-master and the king's presentation of gifts with flirtatious banter (Kotraiah 2003: 107). **they counted us again:** Based on Paes (FE: 284–9). **near the palace walls:** FE: 376. **'state of their king':** FE: 278. **supervised the whole affair:** FE: 268. **elaborate rituals:** FE: 378. **'not a single blow misses':** FE: 266. cf. Nunes claims that 'the first day they kill nine male buffaloes and nine sheep and nine goats, and thenceforward they kill each day more, always doubling the number; and when they have finished slaying these beasts . . .' FE: 377. **his native Lisbon:** FE: 278. **state and religious functions:** Paes goes on to recount many details, for example he describes all the women in attendance. In addition to the hundreds of dancing girls, there were the king's wives and all their personal retainers. Other women were employed as wrestlers, astrologers, singers and soothsayers. There were women accountants who wrote down expenses, others who were cooks and yet others who were judges, bailiffs and sentries (FE: 382–3, 249). **supported by other women:** FE: 273–4. **ate at midnight:** FE: 274. **water sports:** For a colourful description of pleasure gardens, water sports, landscape architecture and hydraulic devices, see Kotraiah 2003: 84. **colourful 'rockets' and fireworks:** FE: 271. **silken cloth of victory:** FE: 271, 378. **colourful trappings:** FE: 381. **specially erected tent:** The description 'tent of Mecca velvet' is unclear. **perfect formation:** FE: 275. **'I was in a dream':** FE: 278–9. **pardaos:** For more details about troop payment systems and officers with their own revenues, see Paes (FE: 280–1). Nunes offers a different reading of the monetary transaction: 'Within these nine days the King is paid all the rents that he receives from his kingdom; for, as already said, all the land belongs to the King, and from his hand the captains hold it. They make it over to the husbandmen who pay nine-tenths to their lord; and they have no land of their own, for the kingdom belongs entirely to the King; only the captains are put to charges on account of the troops for whom the King makes them responsible, and whom they are obliged to provide in the way of service' (FE: 379, cf. FE: 283). **Vijayanagara mint:** The Vijayanagara empire struck many gold coins that were valued throughout the Deccan and south India. The foundations of the centralized royal mint can still be seen today among the ruins of the royal enclosure in Hampi.

15. The Final Years

several waterworks: Earlier in his reign Krishnadevaraya built a great dam and channel at Korragal, and another canal at Basavanna, both of which Sewell claims were in good use and of great value during his time (FE: 162). cf. description of tanks and water sheds (Kotraiah 2003: 20–2). ***dharma* will grow:** AM IV.236. **intricate piping system:** FE: 364–5 and Note 1; Nunes notes that when the king's brahman priests advised offering blood sacrifices to bless the project, 'the King sent to bring hither all the men who were his prisoners, and who deserved death, and ordered them there to be beheaded; and with this the work advanced'. **'a great worker in stone':** 'Portuguese visitors early in the sixteenth century were surprised to note the absence of the use of lime mortar in building construction' (Habib 2016: 104). But perhaps the Portuguese didn't fully realize what native engineers were doing since using lime was an ancient Indian practice (thanks to Professor Michel Danino for pointing this out). Indeed, by Vijayanagara times, Indians had developed a complex system of hydraulics including the management of monsoon rains with rain harvesting tanks, canals, aqueducts, stone channels, drains, wells and dams. Habib adds, 'From the rich epigraphic evidence we have on the matter, it is clear that while a powerful "despotic" state might have been necessary for the lager irrigation works, for most local or village irrigation tanks, and sluices and canals, the dominant rural elements had developed traditional customs and practices by which the works could be constructed and maintained' (Habib 2016: 98). **envoy a private audience:** FE: 350. **'kiss my foot':** FE: 351–2. **growing megalomania:** In reference to this self-aggrandizing personality trait, Narayana Rao and Shulman comment on Krishnadevaraya's boastful colophons: 'The same self-confident, brazen excess runs through each of his verses and the book as a whole' (Narayana Rao and Shulman 2002: 43). **'sudden fits of rage':** *grandes supitos* as Paes calls them. FE: 247. **'kiss-my-foot demand':** Aiyangar questions much of Nunes's account of the battle of Raichur and its aftermath. He adds 'the phrase "kissing the foot" is more Mussalman in character than Hindu, and means no more humiliation than a surrender at discretion' (Aiyangar 1941: 167–8). **'path of rain clouds':** AM V.161. **'rise to kiss the sky':** AM VI.139. **'kingdom of Deccan':** FE: 353. **ransacked the city:** FE: 353–4. **razed the fortress to the ground:** FE: 357. **Bahmani sultan Mahmud Shah:** FE: 358. **'together against the king':** FE: 358. **'found in most textbooks':** Eaton 2008: 308. **'heroic, virtuous, pious, and just':** Eaton 2008: 307. **'god Krishna born again into the world':** Kesava Rao 2000: 243; cf. AM I.31. **either peace or war:** FE: 358. **son of his chief queen Tirumaladevi:** Tirumalaraya was born on 15 July 1518 and died in 1524. For more on Krishnadevaraya's wives and children, see Sistla 2010: 86–8. **son as the new king:** For a rich description of the *abhishekam* of a *yuva-raja*, from the Kannada *Dharmanatha*

Purana, see Kotraiah 2003: 42–3. **fell sick and died:** FE: 359. **beloved minister Timmarasu:** Aiyangar maintains that the guilty party was the minister Timmappa Dannayaka, one of Timmarasu's sons (Aiyangar 1941: 169). **'poisoned my son':** FE: 359–60. **'they remain alive':** FE: 360–1. **one eye open:** AM IV.241. **'die all the kings of Vijayanagara':** FE: 362, perhaps a reference to hereditary prostate cancer. Based on a reading of the inscriptional archive, 'it seems certain therefore that KDR death occurred between October 27 and December 28, 1529' (Sewell 1932: 245). **like a living corpse:** *jivacchavamban* from chatu verse, cf. Narayana Rao and Shulman 2002: 157. **Lord Rama himself was ruling:** AM I.34. **the two are one:** cf. AM IV.270: 'A king should care for the empire like his own body for the two are one. He should consult physicians, as he does ministers and cut back on feasting, as well as taxes. He should strengthen his muscles and reduce his fat, knowing the parts of his body like the wealth in his land. He should be oiled, massaged and bathed clean as if crushing and eliminating his enemies. He should maintain a good complexion and care for his teeth like a well-ordered society headed by brahmans. The king should never forget to keep good health for affecting his body affects the empire.' **'welfare of the king':** AM IV.204–5. **'blossoming kingdom':** Purananuru 186 translated by A.K. Ramanujan (Ramanujan 1985: 158). **'not mine':** Hultzcsh in Burgess 1892: 398–401. **'even after his death':** Kotraiah 2003: 33. **sun and moon shall endure:** Hultzcsh in Burgess 1892: 402. **'do the best you can':** AM IV.276 and AM IV.284.

A Note on the Author

Srinivas Reddy is a scholar, translator and musician. He studied classical South Asian languages and literatures at UC Berkeley and currently teaches at Brown University and IIT Gandhinagar. Srinivas is also a concert sitarist and spends his time performing, teaching and conducting research around the world. His previous books include translations of Krishnadevaraya's *Amuktamalyada* and Kalidasa's *Meghadutam* and *Malavikagnimitram*.